the
Mermaid
METHOD

the MERMAID METHOD

A Lifestyle Designed to Unleash Your True Spirit

GENNAH NICOLE

NEW YORK

LONDON • NASHVILLE • MELBOURNE • VANCOUVER

the Mermaid METHOD

A Lifestyle Designed to Unleash Your True Spirit

© 2021 Gennah Nicole

Published in New York, New York, by Morgan James Publishing. Morgan James is a trademark of Morgan James, LLC. www.MorganJamesPublishing.com

ISBN 9781631953156 paperback
ISBN 9781631953163 eBook
Library of Congress Control Number: 2020945255

Cover Design by:
Megan Dillon

Interior Design by:
Melissa Farr
melissa@backporchcreative.com

Morgan James is a proud partner of Habitat for Humanity Peninsula and Greater Williamsburg. Partners in building since 2006.

Get involved today! Visit
MorganJamesPublishing.com/giving-back

To my shooting star, Sean Moses,
thank you for teaching me how to LIVE.

Contents

Acknowledgments

This book could not have been possible without the undying love and support surrounding me.

Thank you to my mother for recognizing the writer in me before I was able to see it in myself. Thank you to my pops for showing me how to shine in the spotlight, and thank you to my brothers for teaching me how to take a punch and deliver a punch line.

Thank you to my publishing agent, David Hancock, and the Morgan James Publishing team for taking a chance on this new author. Thank you to my editors, Cortney Donelson, Ashley Brooks, and Kristal King for catching my mistakes and helping me to become a better writer.

Thank you to all my sea sisters near and far, especially my Ekela Mermaids for encouraging me through this dream and always being down for a dance party. Also to my HB Mermaids for welcoming me into your pod with open arms and helping me get the hang of this professional mermaid world.

Many mahalos to my writing mentor, Hugette Montesinos-Rodriguez, I appreciate you for bringing my writing voice to life and always sharing your inspirational energy. A big thank you to Taylor Kasha for introducing me to The Universe and showing me how to appreciate all its magic.

And above all else, thank you to *you* for feeling called to pick up this book. I hope these words give you all the motivation and inspiration you are looking for.

Introduction

So You Want to be a Mermaid?

Mysterious, alluring, and passionate, with their stunning hair, glowing skin, and killer pair of seashells—I think the real question here is, *who doesn't want to be a mermaid?*

Long before the Disney debut of *The Little Mermaid* in 1989, these mesmerizing sea sirens have captured the hearts of humans everywhere. Now, in our modern-day era, the popularity of and desire for mermaids has become an iconic staple of society. With stylish crop tops that protest "I'd Rather Be a Mermaid" and an endless supply of "Mermaid hair" tutorials to surf through on the Internet, it is no secret that women everywhere are going to great depths to embody these legendary goddesses. But take it from a professional, mermaid life requires a lot more work than watching a couple of YouTube videos and swimming around like a pro in a high-priced silicone tail. It goes far beyond how fabulous your hair is or how big your seashells are because being a mermaid isn't about how you look, it's about how you live.

**So if you want to be a mermaid,
it's time to start *acting* like one!**

The essential nature of a mermaid represents a fierce and fiery spirit. She possesses a heart brave enough to chase adventure and strives to make the most of each new day. Mermaids show appreciation for all they have been blessed with, but for some reason, their ambitious selves always yearn for more. They exude a sense of confidence, courage, and compassion to the world around them while inspiring others to believe. Their carefree spirit and magical energy touch upon a truth that resonates deep within us all. Perhaps these beauties are just what we need to escape the stress and sorrow of our modern world.

As the wise crab Sebastian once said, "The human world . . . it's a mess," and I couldn't agree with that Caribbean character more. Right now, we are experiencing an era where the pressures of being human are demanding. Expectations are at an all-time high as we try to juggle a career, a social life, a happy home, and a banging body. We are so focused on the outward perception of what life should look like that we are slowly breaking ourselves down from the inside. Mental illnesses, including anxiety and depression, are poisoning our minds and feeding into our fears. But of course, humans are too distracted by the digital dimension to even look up and notice what is happening in the present moment. Between global pandemics, racial injustices, and never-ending political debates, we are currently experiencing a great deal of hate and harm in our society. Not to mention, the earth is slowly collapsing because Mother Nature is screaming out for nurture. Now, I'm not telling you to ditch the drama of the human realm and join me where life is in the bubbles since we have no troubles under the sea. Although, I do believe tapping into your mermaid spirit will help you possess the power to bring more love and light into this cold, dark world.

For decades, myths and folklore have presented these glowing spirits as wise women with the power to teach, heal, and guide human beings, which is, ironically, why I am here. It is my soul's intention to guide you through your own transformational journey while creating a life true to yourself, just like I did once upon a time.

Before I became the motivating mermaid I am today, I was just a girl with the hope to become something more. At the ripe age of twenty-three, I broke up with my long-term love, quit my writing internship at FabFitFun, and ran away to an island, alone in the middle of the Pacific. At the time, my main motive for moving to Hawaii was the warm waters and year-round tan, but little did I know, the cosmos had a bigger plan for me.

After cashing in on my one-way ticket to paradise, I found myself lost above the clouds, dreaming of all the possibilities life had in store. In that magical moment, I was gifted with the freedom to become anything I wanted, but the only problem was, I had no idea what I even wanted to be! This life-altering experience really challenged me to dig deep and unveil the core of who I am. As I settled into my new home of Hawaii, I started to embrace the strange sense of solitude and began to create a life true to myself. I found my voice through journaling, connected with my intuition by meditating, and pursued my passions by doing more of what makes me happy. These routine rituals and personal revelations eventually evolved into my signature way of life, which I call *The Mermaid Method*.

So what exactly is The Mermaid Method? Well, I'm glad you asked. The Mermaid Method is a lifestyle designed to transform your mind, body, and spirit. It was created to help unleash your true self and become the best version of you possible! To me, that is a mermaid, but to you, that could be something else. Perhaps it's a fabulous flamingo that makes heads turn with your bright personality, or it's a magical unicorn that believes in the power of possibility, or maybe even a fierce lioness that pounces at any challenge put before its path.

**Whatever your soul aspires to become,
I am here to help you bring it to life!**

I have coached unique individuals from all walks of life; mermaids ranging from age six to sixty, and yes, even a couple of mermen. I've witnessed these phenomenal souls transform into lovers of life, radiating an aura of happiness. So if you are feeling the urge to make a change or take a risk and hope to find your soul, let this guide be a resource for you. You will receive a wakeup call at some point in your life that pushes you to dig deep and discover what happiness means to you. Once you get a crystal clear vision for what that looks like, then the real fun begins, as you are expected to live it out, by the action you take and the choices you make.

Throughout the pages of this book, together we will work toward building healthy habits, discovering your passions, and reconnecting with your childhood spirit by learning how to believe in yourself. This lifestyle method will teach you the value behind staying true to yourself and listening to your intuition while encouraging you to leave a spark of inspiration in today's world. Fueled by my personal pursuit toward mermaid success, this guide was created to help you achieve a life far beyond your wildest dreams. It is not hard to become a glowing spirit that radiates light, love, and pure joy! All you have to do is follow these simple steps, and watch as you transform into whatever your heart is yearning to be. Trust me, I'm a mermaid.

Now let's dive in, shall we?

Chapter 1

Welcome to Another Fabulous Day in the Life of a Mermaid

*I*n the life of a mermaid, every day is a celebration!

We rise with the sun, eat cake for breakfast, and believe the best is yet to come. We understand that with each new day, there is the chance to begin again, an opportunity to learn, a time to grow, and a moment to experience all of the magic that life has to offer.

But maybe you don't get amped up at the thought of a new day. Maybe to you, most days are *just another day*, but guess what? The way your future plays out depends on how you spend each and every day. A solid day helps set the tone for a solid week, which becomes a solid month, then a solid year, and eventually, a solid life. Although it's easy to get caught up in your goals, plans, or expectations for what is to come, you have to pull yourself back to the moment and learn how to experience each day to the fullest. How you choose to live each day is what leads to the creation of it all. Our days are the moments that make up our journey as a whole, so if you want to have the kind of life that radiates happiness, start by waking up and making today fabulous!

Seize the day with a spark of hustle in your heart, make a conscious effort to do more of what makes you happy, and develop personal practices that keep bringing you back to the moment. I know mermaids have the reputation to be more go-with-the-flow kinds of characters. However, a true mermaid knows how important daily rituals are for her wellbeing.

Your lifestyle is your foundation.

It is an everyday routine that keeps you feeling present, centered, and grounded. Regardless of how many times you begin to feel a little lost, establishing a lifestyle fuels your daily grind with direction, helping you find a way back to happiness. It's an anchor that provides you with the structure needed to build momentum and continuously conquer your days.

When it comes to cultivating your lifestyle, consistency is key. At first, it will be challenging to develop the discipline needed to remain consistent in your choices, but it is necessary to keep getting back up any time you fall off the wellness wagon. When you repeatedly show up for yourself and trust the process, these mannerisms will eventually become second nature. Then, as the days pass and you begin to look back, you will be able to see how the little things ended up making such a big difference in the story of your life.

Either you run the day, or the day runs you. So what are you waiting for, sea sister? The sooner you learn how to make the most of your time, the sooner you can start living the life of your dreams. Here are the daily patterns and practices that will help you cultivate the mermaid lifestyle, so you too can begin making every day fabulous!

Skip the Snooze

How many times have you rested your eyes with the thought of "just five more minutes?" Did that choice lead to you scramble out of the house in a frenzy because those extra five turned into an extra forty-five? As tempting as it may seem, hitting the snooze button sets the tone for a never-ending day of playing catch up. The extra time spent snoozing could have been focused on something that would help set the tone for a positive day, such as enjoying a nourishing breakfast, squeezing in a quick sweat, or relaxing in a long, steamy shower. And before you start to get defensive and try to justify it by explaining that snoozing helps with your chronic exhaustion, think again. Every time you slip back into a slumber your brain hits the reset button on your sleep cycle, cueing up the resting process all over again. Then, when your alarm goes off for a second time, you are at an even earlier stage of your cycle, which happens to be a deeper sleep. At this point, you feel forced to drag yourself out of bed, resulting in a groggy and moody mindset for the day. To ensure you don't drift back into dream world, place your alarm in a spot that is difficult to reach. The act of physically getting "up and at 'em" will wake your body and mind. It will help you think twice before crawling back into bed.

And while we are on the topic of alarm clocks, setting the tone for your day starts with the actual tone! If you have one of those cringe-worthy alarm tones that sound like someone sunk your battleship, allow me to suggest a light-hearted melody that triggers a more positive ambiance. Think chimes, bells, or classical guitar. Basically, anything that will start your day with feelings of peace and tranquility.

Although the snooze button can be enticing, it is not worth the frenzy. I know this may sound cheesy and is certainly an overused adage, but "when you snooze, you lose." Keep that mantra in mind the next time you are tempted to crawl back into a deep sea of blankets to pick up where you last left off in a dream about the dude next door. Instead, use that extra ten minutes to chat with him in real life. Like I said, you snooze, you lose.

Have a "Mini-Meditation"

Meditating first thing in the morning is a powerful way to prepare for the day ahead. So if you must hit the snooze because you want to savor every second in your cozy bed, then I recommend you dabble in a "mini-meditation." Try setting your snooze for five to ten minutes, and use this window of time as a chance to connect with your breath, tune in to how you are feeling, and give thanks for all that you have. Starting your day with a moment of silence will help you fall into a harmonious flow. You will feel peace in your overall presence and possess more patience for the situations you cannot control. Your mind will be in the right headspace to make conscious choices by connecting to your intuition at the beginning of your day. Morning meditations will also give you more energy, alertness, and clarity to handle what needs to be done. We will dive deeper into the topic of meditation later on in the book, but for now, try swapping your snooze for a few minutes of stillness and tune into how it sets your tone for the day.

Make Your Bed

Do you recall those hissy fits you would throw as a child when mommy dearest would kindly ask you to make your bed? Growing up kicking, screaming, and straight-up refusing to accomplish such a simple chore has influenced us to underestimate the potential for happiness that comes from making your bed. Every time I let people in on my morning tradition of sprucing up the sheets, they always follow up with the unenthusiastic question, "What's the point?"

Sorry to be the echo of your mermaid mother, but I am about to preach the importance of straightening up your sleep zone. I believe your space is a reflection of self, and if you are looking to discover peace amongst the chaos of life, start by making your bed every morning. Clutter on the outside is a constant reminder of how scattered and unorganized you might be on the inside, and no one likes being around a hot mess. An unkempt bed has the power to drag you down and may even drag you back into its warm embrace. Developing the habit of making your bed first thing in the morning helps you resist the temptation and convenience of jumping back into your bed. Studies have shown that by taking the time to straighten out your tangled mess of blankets and pillows provides an instant boost to daily productivity. Although the chore may seem minor, you can't help but feel empowered by the spirit of accomplishment, and you will carry that feeling with you, creating a ripple effect of efficiency throughout the day.

According to Charles Duhigg, author of *The Power Of a Habit*, simple keystone habits, such as making the bed, are catalysts for other productive behaviors. Making the bed sparks a feeling of success every morning, one that you will continue to carry throughout the day. And if you just so happen to experience one of those "epic fail" kind days, you will come home to the comfort of a bed that reminds you tomorrow is a fresh start. I guess at the end of the day, it doesn't matter which side of the bed you wake up on, what matters is that you made it.

Rise with the Sun

We are beings of nature, which means our internal clocks are connected to the light from our radiant sun. If you want to connect to the world around you on a deeper level, you have to sync up with the earth's daily rhythm. There are many factors that can affect our biological clocks, but light is the most responsive when it comes to triggering the brain to get going. The invigorating energy of daylight gently pulls you out of slumber, and it supports a healthier balance throughout the day. Try facing your bed directly toward the window where the light can shine through in the morning, and whatever you do, please avoid those terrible blackout curtains.

If your mermaid heart resides in a place where the skies stay dark or it's routinely cloudy, when the time comes to rise for the day, I suggest you invest in a wake-up light (yes, they actually make those). This style of alarm clock is made to stimulate the sunshine, causing you to wake up in a gentle, more peaceful way. I also encourage you to open the windows. As you begin to feel the warmth peak through your bedroom, the chirping birds will softly serenade you, a personal wakeup call from nature (or maybe the gardener). Either way, it is time to get up and get moving.

Stop the Scroll

I am not going to act like a saint and tell you I wake up and avoid checking my phone in anticipation every morning because I am not perfect—I am human (actually, I am a mermaid, so that's debatable). However, I do know that when I begin the day by checking my emails, responding to text messages, and scrolling through Instagram, I feel more anxious, stressed, and self-absorbed. We are all guilty of reading social media, our modern-day newspaper, but connecting with it first thing in the morning has a way of feeding our egos rather than feeding our souls. From the moment we unlock our phones, we are hit with an overload of stimulation that sucks us into a black hole of endless scrolling and constant comparison. Then, when we look up and realize how much time was wasted in the digital world, we find our mornings have passed without ever taking a moment to assess how we really feel. Unfortunately, this habit has become an automatic action of our sneaky subconscious. So if you wish to overcome the temptation, try turning off all notifications or sleeping with your phone on airplane mode. You can also keep your phone in a different room and grab it on your way out the door. Do whatever works best for you. Just be sure to give yourself some time to wake up before you pick up the phone and start scrolling.

Set an Intention

Our thinking creates our reality, so it is crucial to gain control of our minds first thing in the morning. Setting a daily intention gives you the ability to choose where you will exert your energy, what thoughts will fill your mind, what foods will fill your body, and how you will spend each day. Intentions are similar to goals; however, they hold important differences. Goals are set for the future and are typically tied to a desired outcome, while intentions are daily actions that are practiced in every moment. Goals require you to plan, prepare, and focus on achieving a specific result, such as becoming a certified yoga instructor or starting your own business. Intentions will keep you rooted in the present by fueling your day with purpose and challenging you to live in alignment with your core values.

When it comes to setting an intention, try not to overthink it. Tune into what your needs and decide on a simple word or a phrase to keep in mind throughout the day. Be sure to write it down somewhere, whether that be on the mirror of your bathroom, on a sticky note in your office, or on the top of your to-do list. That way, every time you catch a glimpse of it, you are reminded to take action in that very moment that will propel you toward your specific purpose. Throughout each day, ask yourself if you are being true to your deepest intentions. If you are not, start doing so immediately, to the best of your ability. Each time you start over by reconnecting to your intention, you are taking one more step toward finding your own authenticity, truth, and happiness.

Remember who you are, make the most of where you are, and trust in all that you are.

Grounding yourself in the moment and living in alignment with your heart's deepest desires will eventually lead to those big-time goals you've set for your future! So don't hyper-focus on the goal setting but start living with intention.

Make Mondays Matter

If you often suffer from the "Sunday scaries," it is time to change your perspective and learn how to make the most of your Mondays. This dreaded day is the most hated, but also the most underrated because with the start of a new week comes an opportunity for new goals, new possibilities, and new victories. It might be hard to get into the swing of things, but Mondays are all about building momentum and approaching the days ahead with a spark of productivity. Tony Robbins, Sir Richard Branson, and even the queen, Oprah, are among the successful people who swear by Mondays. I know it's a lot easier to overcome the Monday blues when you have a private island or a net worth of $2.8 billion, but their Monday mindsets are what led them to the success they have reached today. They believe this day is crucial when it comes to establishing priorities, staying on top of goals, avoiding procrastination, and focusing. If you want to make Mondays suck a little less, try setting attainable goals for the week—go to bed on Sunday at a decent hour, wake up Monday morning with enough time to eat a healthy breakfast, and start the day by doing something special. How you feel about Monday is entirely up to you. Maybe Mondays don't suck after all. Maybe what really sucks is your perspective.

Shake Your Seashells

If you follow me on "the gram," then you already know morning dance parties are my jam. Forget the double shot of espresso. Nothing gets me more hyped in the a.m. than turning on some tunes and waking my body up with a little shimmy and shake. Dancing is a spellbinding power that makes your spirit soar while bringing a boost of cheerfulness into the day. I am proud to confess that I rock out to a dance party regularly, and saying dancing has changed my life is an understatement.

This happy habit helps you conquer the day in a more energized and open-minded way. The more time you spend shaking it out in the morning, the more time you spend triggering your brain to open up the feel-good floodgates. Not only does dancing release endorphins, boost endurance, and improve coordination, it also helps us connect to the feminine energy flowing from within. It has a way of making us feel sexy in our skin and beautiful in our bodies, resulting in more confidence and gracefulness.

Or maybe dancing leaves you feeling the exact opposite? Maybe you are too embarrassed to get down with it, or maybe you have convinced yourself that you are a horrible dancer? I am curious. When did you begin believing that BS? A lot of us feed into insecurities that keep us from doing the things that feel good in our bodies! I am not asking you to shake it out like Beyoncé during a Super Bowl halftime show. I just want you to get out of your head and connect with your body. As a matter of fact, forget any steps or routines. I am challenging you to get in front of a mirror and open up to the awareness that you are here, alive, and in your beautiful body.

Follow along to these simple steps to help you get grooving every day!

1. *Crank up your favorite feel-good song.*
2. *Get in front of a mirror.*
3. *Now shake it.*

Clothing is optional, but not recommended. Sorry if I am coming off too strong, but it is important to feel sexy if you wish to carry yourself with confidence throughout the day. I know it might seem a little awkward at first, but I am inviting you to turn on some tunes and dance—right here, right now. Search The Mermaid Method on Spotify for playlists full of my favorite tracks to which you can shake it out. Practice makes perfect, so get used to waking and shaking every morning. Really focus on connecting to the inner rhythm of your body, and notice how it helps you fall into an ongoing rhythm for the rest of the day.

Tackle Your To-Do List

To-do lists are an essential way to get your life together because they provide your day with a sense of direction. Glancing over a game plan first thing in the morning helps you envision the day, helps you ensure you're making the most of your time, and helps you stay on top of your stuff.

When it comes to incorporating this life-hack into your lifestyle, I have learned it works best to plan out your day the prior night. Right before I gear up to hit the sack, I jot down what I need to get done the following day. The simple act of putting pen to paper helps clear my mind of tomorrow's worries, allowing me a quality night's rest.

Another to-do list tactic I swear by is making your first effort of the day be something you love to do. Thanks to Mark Twain's "swallow the frog" advice, a lot of successful people preach the opposite. The method that Twain made popular claims that if you "eat a live frog first thing in the morning, then nothing worse will happen to you the rest of the day." While I do agree that getting the unwanted burdens out of the way first frees you from the drama of overwhelm, I strongly believe the first moments of your morning should be used to take care of your own wellbeing. Preparing your to-do list with a task that satisfies your soul, such as going for a morning walk, journaling, or even enjoying a warm matcha latte will help you begin the day cultivating a sense of accomplishment. Then, as you check off each duty of business, you can notice the progress of your performance, eventually gaining enough momentum to continue kicking butt throughout the day/week/month/ year. So yeah, sorry not sorry Mr. Twain, but I don't see the point behind eating a frog first thing in the morning when you can have a matcha latte and still be successful.

Leave Space for Magic

While it is important to have a game plan for your day, it's also important to expect the unexpected. Life doesn't always go according to plan and that's okay. When your expectations lead your behavior to become overly obsessed with a specific outcome, or if you're too focused on the future, you miss out on the mini-miracles being gifted to you every day. Allow yourself to "go with the flow" of the day and always remember to say yes to fun! Don't feel guilty if you decided to join the girls for some happy hour "margs" instead of hitting the gym, and don't feel like you *must* accomplish everything on your to-do list to call the day successful. Having a sense of control over certain situations gives us clarity, certainty, and consistency, but it also closes us off to memorable experiences, incredible opportunities, and serendipitous circumstances. We get so caught up in our own idea of how life should be, we forget that life is on its own agenda, and guess what? It is usually way better than what we have lined-up for the day! I understand it can be challenging to free yourself from controlling tendencies and fill your heart with faith, but trusting in the greater plan is what life is all about!

Reflect on the Day

There is a difference between living in your past and looking back on your past. Self-reflection is a personal practice that gives you new perspectives while bringing more awareness to what is and what is not working in your life. It teaches you to learn from your mistakes, celebrate your victories, and turn your days into beautiful memories. When you make reflection a priority in your daily routine, you can make sense of certain situations, track progress with your personal goals, live with more intention, inspire self-acceptance, discover big breakthroughs, and establish a deeper connection to yourself.

To do this, take some time before bed to jot down pivotal moments in your day that brought you joy, gave you hope, triggered pain, challenged your perspective, or helped you understand something a little differently. Shine light on what you did great, as well as what you could have done better, and how you can start living in alignment with your authentic self. Cultivating this habit does not have to be hard. It can be as simple as journaling a sentence related to something that made the day special for you. So many of us are so focused on moving forward with our lives, we forget to look back on the growth that happens with each passing day. Self-reflection is a time to go inward and check in with how we are doing physically, emotionally, and spiritually.

Read Before Bed

When we were younger, many of our bedtime routines revolved around storytime. Some of us snuggled up with one or both of our parents as they told us tales of mystery, magic, and romance. Now in our older age, we might complain about how reading is boring. I have actually had people confess that it is such a snore; it literally puts them to sleep. With as much as I would love to challenge that opinion, I couldn't agree more, which is why I have reconnected with this childhood tradition and re-incorporated reading into my bedtime routine.

Rather than stimulating your mind with a Netflix marathon or social media scrolling, try relaxing your brain by reading. A highly-cited study led by Dr. David Lewis at the University of Sussex in England in 2009 found that reading for as little as six minutes is sufficient to reduce stress levels by sixty percent, slowing heartbeat, easing muscle tension, and altering the state of mind." Getting lost in a good book helps your mind enter an imaginative consciousness, which means . . . get ready for some trippy dreams. All joking aside, this powerful benefit is a prominent way to prepare your mind for a restful night's sleep. Reading before bed can also boost your brainpower, broaden your vocabulary, sharpen your focus, and get your creative juices flowing. Keep a book at your bedside and when you are ready to start winding down from your day, get comfortable, and get reading.

Do Your Best

Not every day is going to be a fabulous one, and that is okay. There will be days when you wake up with zero energy, followed by moments where you are moody and times when your patience is tested. Always remember to check in with yourself and make a mindful effort to do what you can with where you are at that very moment. Keep showing up and putting in the work, regardless of how tired you are, how frustrating certain situations can be, or how far you have to go. Do not let your excuses influence your actions, but rather, continue making choices that align with the life you wish to lead!

As the wise Maya Angelou once said, "Do your best until you know better, then when you know better, do better." And that, my dear sea sister, is the beautiful cycle of personal growth. Free yourself from your old patterns and celebrate the fact that with each passing day, you are committed to becoming the best version of you possible! Then, as you begin to build the foundation of your daily lifestyle through these little quirks of bed making, intention setting, and seashell shaking, I want you to believe that your best will eventually become better than what it used to be. Trust that your efforts will be rewarded and with each passing day, life will become nothing less than fabulous!

Chapter 2

Make Healthy a Habit

*D*on't let the fin fool you; believe it or not, this mermaid is one *shell* of a runner.

As a matter of fact, I ran my first full marathon without any training! *Zip. Zero. Zilch. Nada.*

It was just two days before the annual Honolulu Marathon when I sparked a conversation with a ten-time finisher and new running buddy. I told him how I had gone for a run earlier that day and it kind of sparked interest to partake in this year's race. After explaining to him the fear-based doubts that filled my mind, he looked me dead in the eyes and said, "You know you will be more upset with yourself if you don't try." That was the moment I knew it was time to Nike up, and just do it.

As I shared the news of this new goal with my tribe, everyone thought I was insane. And quite frankly, I don't blame them. We are talking 26.2 miles here; maybe I was crazy to take on a big challenge with so little preparation. But what some call crazy, I call passion. No one could really comprehend how much I enjoyed running, and this race was the ultimate way for me to put my passion to the test. I signed up by purchasing an entry bib off of a craigslist ad. Then I spent my evening making an epic running playlist and eating as much pasta as possible. Just because I skipped out on training didn't mean I would let myself miss out on the carb-loading. They say it is a crucial part of the preparation process, and even though I had no control over what was going to happen, at least I had control over my carbs.

When the clock struck 5:00 a.m. on race day, I slipped into my favorite pair of spandex, anxiously pinned on my number, and headed out to the starting line. That was when it hit me. *I am about to run a freaking marathon!* Despite my lack of taking part in a real training regimen, I was actually excited to embark on the daunting course. There I was, lost in a sea of 25,000 other hopeful athletes, not really knowing what to expect. *Are my toenails going to fall off? What if I have to poop? Will I be able to walk after this?*

Before I knew it, sparks of fireworks lit up the dark dawn sky to signal the start. I set off for the long road ahead by putting one foot in front of the other and left all my worries in the dust. The adrenaline kicked in, and I felt so alive at that moment. Mile by mile, I noticed my heart beating faster and my breath growing deeper as I pushed myself toward these new distances. Then somewhere along mile twenty-two, my body began to shut down. My legs lost all feeling, I got hit with a killer side cramp, and my booty was chafing like no other. Physically, I wanted to give up. Mentally, that was not an option. I knew that running was a game of mind over matter, and the only way I would get through this was by using my thoughts to motivate my body. I continued to put one foot in front of the other until I saw the finish line from a distance. That was when my heart took over, and I found the strength within to sprint all the way through to the end!

I am telling you, runner's high is real. Not just because I had a mean case of the munchies after the race but also because I was totally stoned from this feeling of self-accomplishment. While crossing that monumental finish line, I have never felt so powerful in my body, able in my mind, and driven in my heart all at the same time. My new running buddy was right—even though I didn't prepare properly, I would have been more upset with myself if I never tried because I would have never known the true strength that lies within me. With that being said, I am not telling you to buy a number off craigslist and attempt to run a marathon tomorrow. No, no, no—I am simply sharing this motivating story to show you that health and habit go hand in hand.

Although I did not have a strict training plan, I knew I was capable. Not because running was a consistent part of my lifestyle, but because I cared for my health both physically and mentally, which left me feeling more than ready to conquer that course. Incorporating healthy habits into your daily routine fuels you with the energy, confidence, and ability to overcome whatever life throws your way. Initially, these behaviors can be hard to develop and often require a big change in perspective. You have to be willing to break old patterns, practice self-discipline, and be accountable for your actions. If you are open to making these sacrifices to better your health, I can guarantee the impact will be transformational. Not just in the physical sense, but you will see changes to your mental health, too. You cannot have a strong body without a strong mind, and once you learn how to master your mindset, you will realize that fitness is actually fun! Do not be surprised if, by the end of this chapter, you are swapping Saturday night hangouts for 6:00 a.m. yoga classes or starting to throw back wellness shots instead of tequila shots.

Here is how to make healthy a habit, so too you can crush this marathon called life!

On Your Mark, Get Set, GOAL.

Before you begin your journey toward a healthy lifestyle, it is necessary to get clear on why you are choosing to prioritize your own wellbeing. The key to staying motivated is having a motive. So whatever your purpose may be, take note of your *why*, and remind yourself of this reason any time you feel the urge to give up on your goals. Because trust me, there will be days when a workout is the last thing you want to do. You will find yourself in moments of doubt, distress, and disappointment. But rather than sabotage yourself with all the excuses in the world, make it a point to empower yourself with reason! Although maintaining a healthy lifestyle is a never-ending course, having a tangible finish line will keep you on track as you develop this new style of living.

Start with Sweat

Once you have a better understanding of your goal, do not let the thought of how far you have to go overwhelm you. I know from my marathon experiences how daunting a race to the finish line can be, but I promise, once you get past the first mile, it ain't so bad. As you set out to incorporate fitness into your daily routine, think of sweating as the starting line to a healthy lifestyle. Commit to moving your body a couple of times a week, and pace yourself by taking time to figure out what works for you. Just like bodies, fitness comes in all different shapes and sizes. What works for me might not do it for you, and that is okay (I totally understand how much people hate running). I could care less if you choose to jog, swim, bike, or blade. It does not matter if you savasana in silence or twerk it out on a pole. All that matters is you get out there and get moving. When stagnant energy builds up in the body, you feel dragged down, groggy, and unmotivated. You have to release this emotional bloat by getting the blood pumping, heart beating, and sweat dripping. Working out elevates your mood with the kind of endorphins that battle against depression and anxiety. Oh, and did I mention it helps keep your hormones in check? We all know how wild those little suckers can get. Sweat sessions should be about maintaining your sanity, not about changing your vanity. Do not worry about the number on the scale or stress about fitting into your skinny jeans. Just keep showing up and sweating. Eventually, you will notice the rejuvenating benefits, which create the momentum and mindset needed to make healthier choices all around.

Accountability is Everything

It is completely normal to skip out on your workout or cave to cravings if you are lacking accountability. This growth tactic eliminates the time and effort you spend on unproductive behaviors by having others help keep you focused on the end goal. When you have a community holding you accountable for your actions, the last thing you want to do is let them down. These are the people that give us the drive to keep showing up and putting in the work when all we want to do is throw in the towel. There are tons of different ways to incorporate accountability into your health journey, so allow me to break them down for you.

+ **Seek Out Support**

   A strong support system is the backbone of almost every success story. Whatever healthy habits you are incorporating into your regimen, life is easier when you have people around you who are rooting for your success. You can find these new fitness friends at your gym, during community yoga classes, or even out and about at Whole Foods. Surround yourself with like-minded people who want to see you succeed, and always remember to be that accountability buddy for somebody else!

+ **Put Your Money Where Your Mouth Is**

   Making a financial commitment to your own wellbeing will motivate you to get your money's worth. It can be anything from buying yourself a fresh pair of running shoes, signing up with a personal trainer, splurging on organic produce, or even investing in a mattress to help you sleep like a princess. You can't put a price on your health, so don't be afraid to drop a little cash on this new lifestyle.

+ **Do It for the Gram**

   Sharing your progress with strangers on social media reminds you to celebrate the tiny victories while helping you track any transformation. There are tons of fitness communities out there that want to cheer for you, check-in with you, and connect with you. Upload some sweaty selfies, share your thoughts, and use all the hashtags you can think of. Then, see who slides into your DM's with the motivation to keep it up!

+ **Walk Your Talk**

Sometimes we are oblivious to the fact that what we are putting out into the world is not matching up with what we really want for ourselves. Instead of saying one thing and doing another, it is crucial that you hold yourself accountable for your actions as well. Take the time to get clear on your fitness goals and wellness quirks. Then live them true through the choices you make.

Treat Yourself, Don't Cheat Yourself

For years, I told myself it was okay to scarf down pizza, French fries, and/or cake because I believed my hard work deserved a cheat day. When in reality, I was only cheating myself. Your body is a powerhouse and works extremely hard for you every day; instead of rewarding it with greasy foods or desserts high in sugar, treat yourself to a fresh meal that leaves you feeling refueled and energized. When you eat right, you feel right—it's as simple as that. Do not let the ketogenic, plant-based, gluten-free trends overwhelm you. All you have to do is fill your plate with nutrient-dense foods that are free of artificial ingredients, preservatives, and additives. Make it a point to shop at your local farmers' market, avoid any ingredients you can't pronounce, and spend more time cooking at home. You do not have to count calories or cut out carbs. This is not about going on a diet or losing weight. This is about respecting yourself enough to nourish your body with that good-mood food.

Making this big of a change in your eating habits will be a bit of a challenge at first, but if you stick with it, your taste buds will begin to crave veggies like the jolly green giant, and over time you, will notice a difference in the way your body reacts to food. Eating clean keeps your mind sharp, energy thriving, and skin glowing. You will feel like your poo doesn't stink, and even if it does—*hey, at least you're going number two*. (Yeah, I just went there.) You would be surprised how many people confide in me about constipation. When they explain all the late-night Taco Bell stops and cheesy gordita crunches I think, "No wonder!" Time to cut the crap so you can take a crap. Just because you have been blessed with a great figure and fast metabolism, does not mean you need to eat like a teenager. I mean, Taco Bell might sound like a good idea when you are coming home from the bars at 2:00 a.m. But trust me—junk will catch up to you one day. It could be your arteries; it could be your saggy tush. Either way, genetics will decide. It is no secret that you are what you eat, so instead of being cheap and cheesy, it is time to focus on fueling your body with all things lean, clean, and green.

I do understand how this can be a lot easier said than done because I have fought my own battles when it comes to eating.

My Battle with Binge Eating

They say admitting is the first step, so here goes nothing. "Hi, my name is Gennah, and I'm a binge eater."

As tough as that was to say, I want to share my story because I know I am not alone in this battle. Binge eating disorder is the most common eating disorder, affecting an estimated 2.8 million people in the United States. You would never know, though, because individuals with this disorder often suffer in silence. It is almost impossible to shake the feelings of guilt and remorse after every time you eat. One second you are enjoying your meal, and then the next second, it is all gone. Many of us zone out while we pig out, while others of us eat to fill a void. What I have learned through my own personal experience is that this disorder goes deeper than a desire to eat—it comes from an emotional imbalance.

Perhaps you are not satisfied with your life, which is why you never feel satisfied after you eat. Maybe you eat in secret because you are hiding parts of yourself from the people around you. Or what if you spoon with Ben & Jerry every Friday night to make yourself feel a little less lonely? If any of these scenarios sound too familiar, it is time to get honest with your eating, bring attention to your patterns, and ask for help. I am no eating disorder therapist, and sometimes I still find myself struggling to put down the fork. But I have learned different ways to heal this self-destructive habit that I hope will help you on your road to recovery.

+ **Practice Mindful Eating**

    Eating is an activity we have been doing since we were born, so it is a natural instinct to hit autopilot when it comes time to chow down. Bringing more mindfulness to your eating is not about chewing slowly or taking smaller bites, it is about directing your undivided attention to the food on your plate. Turn off the TV, log out of social media, sit down at the dinner table, and tune into the taste. Allow yourself to be fully present to experience the true pleasure of eating!

+ **Use Chopsticks**

    These utensils can be intimidating to use, but they have been proven to prevent overeating. The stomach gets full before your brain releases the signal to "stop eating." Therefore, the majority of people stuff themselves to the point of discomfort. Using chopsticks helps to slow down the eating process while limiting your intake, allowing yourself to feel satisfied rather than stuffed.

+ **Prioritize Portion Control**

Being a control freak is never a good thing, except when it comes to rationing out your meals. Part of the reason people tend to overeat is because they pack their plates with more food than they need. Since your eyes are bigger than your stomach, try using smaller dishes. That way, you already feel satisfied by looking at a loaded plate.

+ **Skip the Snacks**

Keeping your kitchen stocked with snacks allows temptation to call your name anytime you pass by the pantry. It is too easy to open up a bag of chips and dust it all in one sitting. Or dig into a pint of ice cream only to find yourself scraping at the bottom of the carton. Do yourself a favor, and avoid the snack aisle until you have a better grip on your binging habits.

+ **Give Thanks**

You don't have to be a devout church go-er to give thanks for the food on your plate. Whether it's Thanksgiving or not, saying grace is a delicate way to appreciate the meal before you, give recognition to the preparation process, and honor all the ways it will nourish your body.

+ **Discover the Root of Reason**
The next time you find yourself rifling through the fridge or fixing up a late-night snack, take a second to recognize why. Is it out of boredom? Is it because you are procrastinating? Have you been feeling lonely? Or are you genuinely hungry? It can also be rooted in the way you were raised. Maybe your mermaid mom would force you to finish your entire plate of food, even though you were full. Or perhaps your dad used to surprise you with doughnuts whenever you were feeling sad. There is always an explanation for your actions, so before you blackout into a binge, consider the root of your reason.

Less Booze, More Booch

"Just come out for one," they said. "It will be fun," they said.

I'm pretty sure we have all been there, caving to the peer pressure by telling ourselves one drink won't hurt. Only to find ourselves actually hurting the next day with shame, regret, and a gnarly hangover. Sometimes, drinking can hinder our growth, but the problem is not the bottle of rosé every #winewednesday or discounted margs for

Taco Tuesday. The problem is that we come from a binge drinking culture where catching a buzz on a casual weekday is the social norm. Drinking is one of those things you never realize how much you actually do it until it is taken out of the equation. In hopes of bringing more awareness to your drinking habits and the effects it has over your health, I suggest you cut back on the booze and sip on some kombucha instead. Relax, you little lush. I am not saying you can't have your rosé and drink it, too. I'm just saying if you want to have a healthy relationship with alcohol, it is important to understand what drives you to drink. Then, when your friends invite you out for "just one," you will be able to say yes to a good time and no to the wine because you are in control.

Stay Thirsty

And since we are on the topic of sipping, let us chat about good 'ole H_2O.

To a mermaid, water is life, but even mermaids struggle to stay hydrated. Sometimes, we get so caught up in our day we forget, and other times it just tastes stale, but it's vital for our vitality. Water (or mermaid juice as I like to call it) does more than just quench our thirst; it keeps our beautiful body functioning properly with its magical healing properties. It has the power to rid our bodies of toxins, regulate our temperature, and replenish our energy.

I mean, just the way it makes our skin glow is pretty incredible.

Water is like the fountain of youth, and if you want to capitalize on this liquid gold, you have to make sure you are drinking enough. When it comes to maintaining proper hydration, the rule of thumb is half your body weight in ounces, which can be tough to do. Here are some ways I find the motivation to keep sipping on that mermaid juice.

+ **Get a Bling Cup**

   Even J. Lo admitted that staying hydrated is hard, which is why you can always spot her with a bedazzled cup. Every time this famous tumbler cup sparkles in the sun, Jenny from the Block is reminded to take a sip. I do not recommend you splurge on such a boujee accessory, but I do think it is effective to find a quality water bottle and keep it with you at all times.

+ **Bubbles are Better**

   Water can be a bit bland, but there is something about fizz that makes you feel fabulous! Swapping your water from still to sparkling helps you cut back on soda, aids in digestion, and even curbs cravings. Just be sure to check your labels for hidden sugars and artificial sweeteners (Pro-Tip: Muddle in your own berries, mint, and lemon juice for some spa water vibes or a nice little mocktail.)

+ **Morning Chug**

  Believe it or not, water can be more energizing than coffee in the morning. Waking up to a cold glass of mermaid juice not only jump-starts your metabolism but also jump-starts your intake for the day. It is a lot easier to hit your hydration goal by starting first thing in the morning instead of waiting around until you are thirsty. Keep a glass bedside so it is ready to go right when you wake up!

Prioritize Your Beauty Sleep

Ever since I was a mini mermaid, I have loved my beauty sleep. No joke, my mom said that once upon a time, I slept for an entire day. Apparently, she had to keep checking on me just to make sure I was still alive. (I guess you can say I have always been a big dreamer.) Still to this day, I prioritize my rest. Obviously, I am not sleeping all day like I used to, but I allow myself to catch up on Zs if my body needs it.

Sleep is a key component to a healthy lifestyle, and like any regimen, it requires dedication. Sleep takes time and you have to set aside at least eight hours of your jam-packed day to reap the rejuvenating benefits it has to offer. Let me tell you, though, it is worth all the time in the world. If you are not well rested, your body becomes more prone to injury, your mind becomes more prone to moodiness, and your eyes become more prone to under-eye circles as ratchet as a raccoon. Pardon me for getting hung up on appearances, but they don't call it beauty sleep for nothing, which could be the reason why you struggle to shed some stubborn pounds. Skipping out on crucial hours of shuteye increases insulin levels, putting you at higher risk for heart disease, diabetes, or even a stroke. So the next time you consider pulling an all-nighter, raging until sunrise, I want you to remember the best kind of party is a slumber party.

Rise and Grind

I know we just talked about the value of sleep, but there is something powerful about waking up early and starting your day with a solid sweat session. As you begin to establish a routine sleep schedule, be sure to set aside the time to get your body moving first thing in the morning. Once you do, notice how your energy increases, your mindset shifts, and your days become better than your dreams!

Not only are you gifting yourself with more stamina to handle serious business, but you are also building the momentum for another fabulous day! I get it, though, sometimes it's hard to get up and get moving. Sometimes, we are groggy, and sometimes we are hung-over. Sometimes, we are in a funk, or sometimes we have zero sense of direction, which is why having a workout planned from the jump-off will help you feel strong, able, and accomplished before your day even begins! Plus, if you wait until the final hours of your day, you are more likely to skip the workout altogether.

You might as well commit to it before your brain is awake and aware of what in the world is actually going on.

To help build this healthy habit, try setting out your workout attire the night before. That way, you are ready to go from the get-go. Or challenge yourself to sign up for a 6:00 a.m. class at your favorite studio, and find a friend who will not let you flake on yourself.

Celebrate Your Silhouette

How crazy is it to think a good portion of my younger years was spent obsessing over a boob job? I mean . . . I grew up in Orange County, California where plastic surgery is a right of passage for a girl, so I guess it wasn't really all that crazy. Lucky for me, I was broke as a joke and struggled to save the $10,000 required to go under the knife. Instead, I accepted my itty-bitty titties and learned how to love myself for all the other assets I was given (emphasis on the *a-s-s*). Although, this kind of compassion can be difficult to have.

According to a 2011 article I read on glamour.com, research indicates that on average, women have thirteen negative body thoughts daily. Meaning, one thought out of every waking hour is focused on judging, comparing, or even despising the beauty of our bodies. And thanks to the rise of social media comparison, I can imagine the average being higher today. Even after years of practice, I still suffer from body image issues like everyone else. Sometimes, I cringe when I catch a glimpse of my cellulite in the mirror, and I have arms with bat wings that would make The Dark Knight jealous. However, through my journey toward tiny titty acceptance, I discovered it's all in our heads (hence the word "self-conscious"). Once we learn how to keep our egos in check, we can lead lives where we feel confident, energized, and at peace with the bodies we have been given. Your incredible body works hard for you every single day. Make sure you honor it for all that it does, rather than picking it apart for all that it is not.

Here are ways you can show your body all the love it deserves and celebrate your silhouette!

+ **Stand Tall, Stand Proud**
Having a solid stance is the first step to feeling confident and revamping your self-image. Start to carry yourself with pride by standing tall, keeping your shoulders back, chin lifted, and a sparkling smile on your face. Tiny tweaks in body language not only change body chemistry but also open you up to more love and opportunity.

+ **Make a List of What You Love**
Instead of looking in a mirror and nagging yourself about the parts of your body you wish were different, try shifting your perspective by making a list of what you love! Don't keep it limited to just your physical

body either. Take note of different characteristics that make you, YOU! Then, you can focus your thoughts on these qualities and let them shine through any chance you get.

+ **Get Naked**

Why cover yourself in clothes when you can find true comfort in your body? Gaining the confidence to strut your stuff in the buff teaches you how to appreciate your body for what it can do, love your body for how it looks, and accept your body for all that it is. Stop hiding behind lounge sets and start living in your own skin.

What's Up Doc?

Have you ever had one of those morbid dreams where your teeth fall out? I used to get them *ALL. THE. TIME.* Waking up in a panic while gliding my tongue from cheek to cheek, making sure my smile was still intact. Google says these nightmares can mean anything from being stressed to being self-conscious about your appearance. I knew mine surfaced for an entirely different reason. When they started to happen more frequently, I was long overdue for a check-up at the dentist and subconsciously, my dreams were nagging at me to make that appointment. When I finally decided to drop in for a cleaning, I immediately regretted waiting so long. There was so much work to be done, and I paid for it (literally).

Make it a point to visit your doctors regularly and get check-ups to ensure all parts of your body are healthy, happy, and working properly (especially while you are still on your parents' insurance). Making it a habit to hit up your doctors keeps you on top of your health game, and you will catch any possible signs of sickness early on. This ensures you can take the needed precautions before it grows into something a little more serious. Routine visits also help give you a better peace of mind knowing that your body is in good condition so you can rest easy at night rather than being haunted by toothless dreams.

Push Past Plateaus

Now let's say you have been doing this healthy thing for a while but you are not noticing any changes in your body, mind, and spirit. Chances are, you have hit a plateau— what marathoners refer to as hitting "the wall." It's when you reach a state of little or no change in your progress. No matter how hard you run, you are getting nowhere, causing you to lose momentum even while moving forward. This can be one of the most frustrating and discouraging stages of any journey toward wellness. Before you decide to throw in the towel, here are a couple of ways to help you find the motivation to hit it a little harder and stay on track with your healthy lifestyle:

+ **Mermaid Melodies**

   Any time I find myself in a running rut, I know it is time to add fresh music to the mix. Spicing up your playlist with new jams is the perfect way to break the bore and get pumped to crush your next workout. I find that trance-y tunes, empowering lyrics, and bass-heavy melodies always set the tone to help me run a little faster, lift a little heavier, and sweat a little harder.

+ **Treat Yo Self**

   If you have been showing up and putting in the work every day, do not hesitate to splurge on some new leggings, invest in the latest Fitbit, or treat yourself to a full-body massage. Not only does your hustle deserve to be rewarded, but these kinds of things will enhance your workouts and wellbeing!

+ **Track Your Progress**

   Logging your progress is a great way to stay on top of your goals while helping you figure out what is and is not working with your regimen. For example, last week you were struggling with finishing ten push-ups, and this week you are banging out twenty, no problem! When you hit a plateau, these are the tiny victories you need to recognize and celebrate.

Try tracking your health journey through different fitness apps, transformation photos, or putting the pen to paper.

+ **Switch the Scene**

Nothing good comes from comfort zones. If you are currently experiencing a peak in your performance, try challenging yourself to something new. Sit in the saddle at a spin class, target tiny muscle groups with a barre-inspired workout, or hit the beach for a stand-up paddleboard session. Giving your body something different to adjust to, forces it to move in new ways, which produces new results.

+ **Be in Your Body**

Once you have been working out for a while, it will begin to feel second nature to you. Rather than showing up to the gym and simply going through the motions, be in your body and feel those muscles work! The slower you move, the more aware you are of your movement, and the more connected you will feel in your body.

+ **Remember Your Why**

Whenever you find yourself stuck in a lull, take a moment to reconnect with your why. Remembering what drives you will re-spark that fire of purpose within, drown any doubt you might be feeling, and remind you that these struggles will lead to success. Don't let a plateau keep you from reaching your finish line. Remember why you started and keep putting in the work sea sister!

Train Your Brain

While many might assume the toughest parts of a marathon are the chaffing thighs or bleeding nipples—they are not. The toughest part of a marathon is mastering your mindset. You see, running is a game of mind over matter. An internal battle between showing up and giving up, challenging you to focus on how good it makes you feel rather than how much it makes you hurt. Every run is an endless pep talk to keep pushing until the end and to be honest, it is hard to achieve that kind of mental strength. When it comes to building a healthy lifestyle, everyone tends to be fixated on the physical aspect, but the truth is, a healthy body is the result of a healthy mind. When you train your brain to believe in your strength, get into the zone and push past your limits, you will be able to turn any obstacle into an opportunity. Studies have proven that building mental strength has the power to enhance performance, maintain motivation, and trust your ability. To achieve this kind of inner excellence, you have to be willing to put in the work. Much like strength training, building mental muscle requires a whole lot of time, energy, and effort. You must keep your focus sharp by eliminating all distractions. It is vital that you visualize success, develop a positive perspective, and maintain resilience. There will be curveballs, setbacks, and failures on your journey, but you have to find the mental toughness to keep going. Trust that you are fierce AF and you are capable of doing whatever you put your mind to, then do the dang thing!

Start Today

There have been so many times on my wellness journey where I would justify my unhealthy choices with, "I'll start tomorrow" or "When Monday comes around, I will get back on my game." I finally realized that mentality was getting me nowhere. Who says it has to be a new day, a new week, or a new year to start living a healthy lifestyle? All you really need is a new perspective.

Every moment is a chance to start again by making choices that align with your ultimate visions and goals. Stop waiting until tomorrow to prioritize your health and start taking action today! You have the resources to help you establish a healthy, active, and vibrant wellbeing. As I mentioned before, don't let the journey to the finish line overwhelm you. The only way to reach the finish line of a marathon is by putting one foot in front of the other. As you set out to build an active lifestyle, take it one day at a time, and trust in your strength, determination, and will power to take you to the finish line. There is no better time than now to start making healthy a habit.

So what are you waiting for? Goal get 'em, mermaid!

Chapter 3

Stay True to You

I am not sure what your love life looks like, but I have been single for nearly a decade.

I mean, it's not as depressing as it sounds. And before you think I am a salty mermaid who has never experienced true love, think again.

In my younger years, I was in a long-term relationship with one of the greatest guys I have ever known. He was the kind of guy that surprised you with flowers, just because. He was always down for spontaneous adventures, and more importantly, he was always down to drive. He let me go out dancing all night with my girls and would hold back my hair whenever I had a little too much fun. He did the dishes, he folded my laundry, and he always saved his last bite of food for me. Now if that is not love, I don't know what is.

So what happened?

Well, that is a good question because letting him go was one of the hardest decisions I ever had to make. I had an amazing man willing to love and care for me, but deep down, I wanted to learn how to do it on my own. Granted, I didn't expect to experience a dry-spell for a decade, but looking back on my single years, I have no regrets. Had I followed the societal timeline, I would have been led down a road of resentment. I would have gotten caught up in planning a fairytale wedding, going on our honeymoon, buying a home, getting a dog, and having a baby.

Because that is what everyone expects of us, right?

At that time in my life, I had no clue what I wanted for myself. I had no idea who I was without my boyfriend, and I definitely didn't know how to take care of myself. How was I ever supposed to take care of a household—or an animal—let alone a newborn baby? As much as I loved this man, I knew I needed to learn how to give that same kind of love to myself. So with a heavy heart, we parted ways, and I began to build an honest, passionate, and committed relationship with me, myself, and I.

I distanced myself from everyone and everything I knew to better understand who I was and what makes me happy. I became selfish with my time and discovered my talents. I stopped seeking approval from others and started accepting myself. This personal quest really turned me into somewhat of an introverted expert, and through this journey of radical self-love, do you know what I discovered? It is a lot harder than famed rapper Lizzo makes it out to be. This personal practice goes way deeper than bubble baths and face masks.

Loving yourself is also about speaking your truth, trusting your intuition, owning up to your mistakes, forgiving your failures, and believing in your beauty. It requires you to be vulnerable, have courage, and show the world who you are! Although fully embracing your independence is a tough thing to do, only through the hardship are you able to recognize your true brilliance. This is when your strengths are brought into the light and the fire within you is ignited. I am convinced that taking the time to connect with the core of who you are is what causes more self-awareness, sparks some serious self-motivation, and helps you figure out the true meaning of self-respect. This trifecta of personal best is what helps us show up in the world as our best selves, which ironically, benefits everyone else around us! It doesn't matter if you are as single as a Pringle or happily married with kids, self-love is a key component to a flourishing life because the most important relationship you will ever experience is the relationship you have with yourself. You can't pressure your partner to snap you out of a bad mood. You can't rely on your parents to always give you words of wisdom. And, you should not wait for someone else to book that two-week Bali retreat you have been dreaming of.

Sorry for the tough love sea sister, but it is not anyone else's job to make you happy—**it is yours!**

Through my single girl stage, I have discovered the only constant in this life is you, and as long as you stay true to your own beautiful self, you will always be able to rely on your love. Stop searching for another person to fill you with affection, acceptance, and reassurance, and start turning to yourself for love, inspiration, and guidance. There is no Prince Charming in this story because—plot twist—you are your own hero! When you learn how to find solace in solitude, embrace your individuality, speak your truth, and make your own choices, you will learn how to create your own happily ever after. Here is how you can stay true to your heart, fill yourself up with love, and turn your life into a full-blown fairy tale.

Practice Social Distancing

Remember that one time the government put us all in a personal timeout? You know, when we were hit with the infamous news that the world has been encouraged to self-quarantine and spend several months in isolation? Talk about setting boundaries. But I must say, I jumped on that "social distancing" bandwagon with no shame because sometimes, we need a little space from others. We often define ourselves by the #squad or communities we belong to, and somewhere along the way of trying to fit in, we lose touch with our own unique energy. Between the media telling us what we should believe, our friends having a say in what we wear, and our family telling us how we should behave, we are easily influenced and distracted by our everyday surroundings, making solitary confinement not a bad idea. Whether it is as simple as a digital detox or as extreme as a full-on quarantine, I do believe keeping a respectful distance between social circles and social media is beneficial to our personal health. It is important to be alone with our own thoughts and get clear on our values to live our most authentic lives. At first, spending time solo might bring up feelings of alienation, boredom, and selfishness, but be mindful of these moments and push past the resistance. Setting boundaries is crucial for your own personal development and the more your honor them, the more aware you will become of your own individual needs.

Be Your Own Bae

I have lived on my own, traveled around the world solo, and even taken pleasure in going to the movies by myself. I don't have a problem making reservations for one, jamming out at concerts alone, or hitting up the single rider line at Disneyland. Some might say I show myself a little too much love, but I believe there is nothing wrong with that! Wanting to hang out with yourself does not make you self-centered; it is how you can show up into the world as the best version of you. Whenever I make it a point to take myself out for a night on the town, I feel rejuvenated in my spirit, reconnected to my heart, and reminded of the courage I carry because let me tell you, dating yourself takes serious guts. It challenges you to walk alone with pride, let go of others' perceptions, and show yourself the kind of love you deserve. Here are different ways to put the effort into dating yourself:

+ **Flower Power**

    A vase of fresh blooms has been proven to enhance emotional health, but you shouldn't wait around for someone to shower you with flowers. Pick up a fresh bouquet of your favorite blossoms to fill your heart with color and bring more happiness to your home.

+ **Wine & Dine Yourself**

    I know showing up to dinner as a "party of one" can be kind of intimidating, but when you overcome that initial fear, you are filled with a strong sense of personal empowerment. I mean think about it. You get to drink as many cocktails as you please and don't have to share the free bread with anyone. Forget about that awkward moment when the server drops the bill and there is zero question about whether or not you plan to order dessert. Do you really think a random Hinge date will ever top that kind of company? Yeah, me neither.

+ **Always Put Out**

I know masturbation is a taboo topic, but it is such an intimate form of self-love. Chances are you have felt the mind-blowing benefits of "The Big O," so I don't have to go too much into detail about how incredible it is to rub one out. But I will tell you this: The power of an orgasm is literally in our own hands, and this kind of self-exploration helps form a deeper connection between you and your body. You don't need a partner to make you feel sexy and sensual, like a true ravenous. All you need is a vibrator.

+ **Leave Yourself Love Notes**

Sometimes, you need to tell yourself just how incredible you really are! Writing yourself little notes of inspiration gives you the ability to feel love on those crappy days when all you need is a hug. Scribble down sentences about how proud you are of your efforts, how brilliant you are in your mind, and how beautiful you are in your own way! Then hang them up around your house, in your car, or at the office. That way, you are always reminded of how loved you are, wherever you may be!

+ **Avoid D*ck-stractions**

Sometimes, men are what I like to call a "D*ck-straction." If we are in a relationship with them, we have a tendency to put their needs before ours, and if we are single, we often find ourselves caught up in the chase. Some guys preoccupy our minds with their bull-crap, so dodge these kinds of dudes at all costs. You do not have to worry about pleasing your partner or finding a boyfriend; keep doing you and the right man will love you for that. He will support you in all your efforts, rather than try to distract you with his D.

+ **Put a Ring on It**

   Once you create an honest, caring, and passionate relationship with yourself, it is time to make it official. Try writing some vows and make a promise to always love yourself. Sometimes, I have even gone so far as to throw myself a ceremony, complete with a Plumeria bouquet, my favorite sundress, and champagne, of course! Only when you learn how to truly love yourself, will you be ready to share that love with another person. Because once you learn how to love all that you are, you will not settle for anything less than what you DESERVE!

Self-Love Versus Self-Care

Self-love and self-care are basically the same things, right? Wrong. While these wellness practices are intertwined, there is a big difference between the two, and you have to understand the distinction to know what your spirit needs. We are going to start by breaking down self-care. This approach to wellness is all about caring for yourself, both physically and mentally. I am sure you make time for the surface level stuff like soothing bubble baths, relaxing massages, and invigorating workouts, but are you making time to care for your mind, too? As necessary as it is to pamper yourself at the nail salon, it is just as important to dabble in some meditation, declutter your space, and unplug for the day. By showing attention to your mental health, you can satisfy your overall wellbeing!

Now that you have a better idea of what self-care entails, it is time to explore the concept of self-love. This sacred ritual represents total self-acceptance. It is practiced by bringing full awareness to your emotional side and having more compassion for yourself. This involves everything from monitoring the dialogue in your head to expressing the confidence you exude. It requires you to know your worth, appreciate your quirks, and recognize that you are enough. Self-love is more of an intuitive art, whereas self-care requires you to take action. One size doesn't fit all when it comes to self-care and self-love. Not everyone feels calm after a massage, just as not everyone finds confidence from the same sources. All that matters is that you spend time discovering what your spirit needs, slow down, and make yourself a priority.

Environment is Everything

They say you are a product of your environment, so I suggest you take a big step back and pay attention to your surroundings. Do you love being home at the end of a long day, or are you on edge because of your roommate's constant mood swings? Are your friends calling you for an early morning workout or tempting you with text messages to join them for some late-night drinks? Does your workplace inspire creativity and imagination, or are you left feeling overworked and exhausted? It is no secret that your current conditions play a major role in the outcome of your life, but what you might not know is this: You are in full control of your surroundings.

I knew that I wanted to live close to the beach, spend my time with people who would inspire me, and have a year-round tan. After getting honest with my ideal surroundings, I decided to rebuild a life for myself in Hawaii. I rented out a quaint cottage one mile from the sand. I formed lifelong friendships with one-of-a-kind souls, and my tan was so on point, even locals thought I was an island native.

You have the power to shape your life however you please! If you are not too crazy about the area you live in, then move. If the company you keep is full of drama and gossip, make new friends. And if your job is not pushing you to your fullest potential, then I suggest you quit. Your environment has an influence over your mood, your habits, and your success. If there is something you don't like in your life, then plant a new seed and create an environment where you will flourish!

Embrace Vulnerability

Vulnerability is something we all fear.

It is intimidating to let our walls down and allow people to see the struggles, insecurities, and worries we work so hard to hide. It is nerve-wracking to share our thoughts, our voices, and our creations for people to judge. And it is scary AF to love someone with an open heart, especially with the fear of rejection or not being fully accepted.

As a result, we avoid vulnerability at all costs.

We go about our lives, refusing to show others who we really are, how we really feel, and what we are really capable of. According to vulnerability guru Dr. Brené Brown, vulnerability is defined as "uncertainty, risk, and emotional exposure." Dr. Brown also claims, "vulnerability is the birthplace of love, belonging, joy, courage, empathy, and creativity." To her expert understanding, "What makes you vulnerable, makes you beautiful," so if you are only putting the best parts of yourself out there for the world to see, then you are going about this vulnerability thing completely wrong. It is about putting it *all* out there, allowing others to love the most real, honest, and authentic version of you. Vulnerability happens by sharing the parts of yourself you are so quick to hide, opening your heart to the sting of rejection, and not being afraid to ask someone for help. The more you start to peel back the layers of yourself, the more you will be able to see the openhearted and fearless fighter within you. Always be on the lookout for any opportunity you have to let your guard down and allow someone to love you for *YOU*!

Use Your Voice

Not to sound like a salty mermaid, but I have always had an issue with Ariel. I just do not understand why anyone would want to give up their beautiful voice in exchange for a nice pair of legs. I cannot blame her, though. Sometimes, it takes losing your voice to understand how valuable it really is.

The only reason I know this is because a similar situation happened to me but on a different level. One time, I competed for the title of Miss Hawaii USA. Leading up to the evening of the pageant, I was doing everything in my power to take the stage with confidence. I was hustling hard to find sponsors, squatting low to look good in a bikini, and working overtime to pay for an overpriced evening gown. I gave that opportunity my best shot, so you can imagine my disappointment when your girl got cut in the first round. However, this blow to the ego is less about losing and more about the lack of publicity. I remember feeling bitter backstage because I was unable to be a part of the on-stage question portion. I didn't sign up for the pageant to prance around and look pretty. I signed up to speak in front of a crowd and show the audience who Gennah really is! I had waited (and literally, worked my booty off) for months for that second in the spotlight, only to have it taken from me—just like that. I hope by now you can see where my issue with Ariel lies. She voluntarily handed her voice over to a sea witch, while mine was stolen, all thanks to the politics of pageantry. Nevertheless, just like Ariel, this humbling experience pressured me to appreciate my voice on a whole new level.

Had I been given the opportunity to speak on that memorable night, chances are I would have answered with something related to "world peace" since that is what the judges usually want to hear, right? How many times have you found yourself saying something to win the approval of others, instead of sharing what you really think about certain situations? Have you ever had to bite your tongue in fear of how the other person would take it? Or even worse, have you ever apologized for something that was not even your fault?

It is easy to be passive and let others speak up on your behalf, but if you don't learn how to use your voice, then you will never learn the power that lies within you. If you tend to be shy, you might miss the chance to share your thoughts, explain to others how you feel, or stand up for what you believe in. Speaking your truth is all about changing your attitude and trusting in yourself that what you are saying is worth hearing. Start by opening up more to your social circles, sharing your thoughts, theories, and wisdom. Get clear on what you are trying to say before you say it. Sometimes expressing yourself can be a bit of a struggle, and there is no problem with taking your time to figure out how you feel and gather the right words to explain your point of view. Also, remember to remain in control of your emotions. When you feel yourself starting to boil with anger over a heated debate, take a step back, breathe, and politely remove yourself from the conversation. There is no need to lose your cool while trying to justify why pineapple belongs on pizza (it just does). Pineapple lover or not, everyone is entitled to their opinions, and you have to agree that effective communication comes from listening with attentiveness, speaking eloquently, and aligning your actions with your words.

Take Up Space

Long before Lebron jumped on the L.A. bandwagon, I landed the audition of a lifetime and took to the court to become the next In-Arena Host for the Los Angeles Lakers. You know, those peppy people that come on the jumbotron between time-outs, challenging innocent spectators to sink a half-court shot for the chance to win an oversized check worth $10,000? Yeah well, I will just cut to the chase and tell you, I didn't get the job. I did, however, get some feedback that has helped me approach life in a whole new way. When I asked why I was not chosen for the coveted position, the decision-makers explained, "You didn't take up enough space to demand our attention." As much as the comment bruised my ego, they were right! We are talking about the house that Kobe built, and if I was going to capture the attention of such a star-studded audience, I was going to have to walk in there with a whole lot of confidence. I was playing with the big boys now, and instead of stepping into the spotlight, I just hung out on the sidelines. I played it way too small and didn't own the stage like I needed to.

Taking up space gives you the power to walk into a room and make heads turn with just your presence. It is about having your words be heard and your energy felt while allowing the confidence within you to shine. Something tells me that you have a lot to offer this world, do not deny us the chance to admire all your glory! Stop holding yourself back by playing it small, and start standing with pride, keep turning heads with your spunk, and try taking up so much space that even Lebron would be intimidated to share the court with you.

Avoid the Vamps

Allow me to compare one mythical character to another.

In one corner, we have mermaids who exude a beauty of warmth. And on the other end of the spectrum, we have vampires who are as cold-blooded as can be. One is full of passion; the other lacks a heart. One is optimistic; the other is a cynic. One is bursting with life, and the other is lifeless. Vampires find energy by feasting on the lives of the innocent, whereas mermaids gain vitality by fueling others with love.

Now that we have established the difference between daydreamer and nightcrawler, I have another question for you. Is there anyone you know that has vampire-like tendencies by sucking the soul right out of you? These are the kind of people who make you feel drained of energy anytime you are together. They make you find things to complain about and drama to feed into. Sometimes they are a bit narcissistic, always finding a way to bring the conversation back to them. And whatever you do, please beware of how they treat others. They might be as sparkly as Edward Cullen on the outside, but you can't let the charm fool you. If their hearts are ugly, then so are their true characters. It is important to keep away from these villains to ensure they don't turn you over to the dark side and make pessimism your new perspective. Keep your garlic close, and send a stake right through their hearts. Gruesome, I know. But the time has come to cut the toxic ties in your life and make space for new connections that support the spirit you are trying to become!

The Choice Is Yours

In 2018, *Psychology Today* reported that on average, you make up to 35,000 choices every day. That's a lot of daily decisions, and with all those choices, you are presented with, how many are supporting your happiness, success, and wellbeing? I am not going to lie. Sometimes, I drink too much, sleep too little, barely hit the gym, and have zero patience for others. The choices I make don't always leave me feeling like my best self, and as a result, I get down in the dumps. The worst part? There is no one is to blame for this #MOOD but me. How you choose to live your day-to-day plays a big role in how your future will unfold. Whether it feels like it or not, you know what kind of choices it takes for you to live your best life. By saying yes to the moments that make you feel good, and saying no to the junk that makes you feel like crap, it is kind of impossible to experience any kind of #MOOD other than bliss. Now that we got that covered, let's break down our choices, shall we?

+ **The Power of No**

   Oftentimes, others tempt us with a night on the town, or we feel like we need to give our time to others. But in reality, saying yes to every invitation that comes our way leaves us feeling drained and emotionally exhausted. Sometimes, saying no is crucial for our own wellbeing. This does not mean I want you to say no to everyone or everything on the regular. This means giving yourself more time to think, ensuring whatever you say "yes" to aligns with the vision you have for yourself. Don't feel obligated to join the girls for brunch if it is not in your budget, and don't jump at every opportunity to hang out with the new guy you have been dating if he is not willing to put forth the effort on his part. Ironically, when you say no to an invitation, you are saying yes to your own needs. I promise that in return for saying no, you will be gifted with more—**more energy, more time, more willpower, and more respect.** Work on strengthening your "no muscle" by politely declining any of the opportunities that do not align with becoming your best self.

+ **Can I Get a Shell YEAH?**

There will always be a million reasons to say no, but when you make a choice with a big "shell yeah!" you are putting it into the universe that you are ready, willing, and able to handle whatever comes your way (even if it does not feel like you are). Saying yes is giving yourself permission to try and fail by putting yourself in the position to accept that not everything goes according to plan. It has the power to attract positivity and abundance while teaching you more about yourself. If you say no to a solo-backpacking trip through Southeast Asia, you will never know how self-reliant you are. If you are hesitant to accept a job offer, then you will never see the talents that others recognize in you, and if you refuse to try sushi, then you may never figure out your favorite food. Saying yes isn't about accepting every offer put before you; it is about pushing yourself to rise up, fall down, and try new things.

How crazy is it that some of us are quick to say, "No," while others of us jump at any chance to say, "Yes!" Whenever you are presented with a choice, remember to always do what is best for **YOU!** Start taking full responsibility for your life by making decisions that align with your highest self. Be mindful of the opportunities you are presented with, and make a conscious vote based on how it will affect you in the long run, rather than on how you will feel in the moment. Now get out there and make good choices!

Let Love In

Although I am currently lacking love from a dude, it doesn't mean I am lacking love in my life. And the same goes for you—relationship or not. A lot of us have an attachment to the idea that love is only found with another person, but that is not the case. Rather than worry about love with a partner, I want you to focus on all the other areas of your life that are bursting with love. Spend some time with your girl gang, call your parents, connect with a community, get lost in nature, work on your relationship with The Universe, smile at strangers, and appreciate all the love that already exists around you. Take a step back and really look at the people that bring joy, light, and encouragement into your life. The ones who idolize how awesome you are. The ones who inspire you to grow, and the ones who want the best for you. It doesn't matter if they are your close friends, crazy family, or even a random stranger on the street; know that you are loved by so many incredible people. But don't let that outshine the love you have for yourself. Stay true to your personal promises, stay true to your unique quirks, stay true to your intuitive guidance, and most importantly, stay true to you.

Chapter 4

Paid to Play

The way I see it, our soul-seeking generation yearns for more than business success; we are craving a life of *purpose*. Yes, we want to make money, but we also wish to have our hard work appreciated, our voices heard, and our unique talents shine. We want the freedom to travel, the inspiration to create, and the power to make a difference by simply doing what we love.

We want to get paid to play.

When I discovered this personal revelation, I was in my early twenties, trying to figure out which career path would bring me the most success. And like every modern millennial going through this kind of a quarter-life crisis, I decided to quit my steady job and travel around the world for a couple of months. During this time of soul searching, I explored new environments, met new people, and learned more about what really fuels my fire. Eventually, when I found myself back in the comfort of my home, I avoided jumping on the job hunt right away. Day-by-day, I was trying to keep the adventure going. I was not ready to give up the feeling of freedom for the sake of money, but a mermaid's gotta eat! So until an opportunity came knocking, I needed to figure out a way to get paid doing what I do best.

Here is where things started to get a little interesting.

If you have ever roamed busy city streets, you surely encountered a couple of kooky characters. I have seen everything from a violin playing Santa to a tiny fedora-wearing Guinea pig. And I know you have come across robotic men covered in twenty cans of spray paint, live graffiti art performances, and comical magic shows. Also, how can we forget the legendary Naked Cowboy that plays his guitar in the middle of Time Square wearing nothing but a pair of hand-painted tighty whities! These entertaining street performers use the world as a stage to showcase their unique talents and share their creative gifts with anyone willing to watch.

Now, as a person designed for the spotlight, this was the kind of entertainment that inspired me, and since I was living in Hawaii at the time, I could not help but wonder what the busy streets of Waikiki were lacking. Then my wild imagination conjured up a way for me to get paid to play. Without any hesitation, I bought my first fin, slipped into costume, and took the stage in the heart of Honolulu with nothing but a smile and a money bucket that read, "I Quit My Day Job And Became A Mermaid."

Enthusiastic tourists, laid-back locals, and children of all ages were stopping in their tracks to take photos, share a shaka, and listen to my story. I was causing traffic jams because the double-decker tour buses wanted to stop and say hello, along with curious pedestrians, jaywalking to get to my side of the street. All the attention I was attracting was kind of crazy; however, the craziest part of all was the fact these kind strangers were actually paying me to be a mermaid! I mean sure, it was only a couple dollars here and there, but it began to add up. The more confident I was in what I had to offer, the more money I made. And now, as you can see, this strange idea that started for fun became a rewarding career path. I have entertained as a mermaid in luxury hotels, cruise lines, private parties, music festivals, and even made it on network television.

But if we are being honest here, my pursuit toward mermaid success has not been an easy one. Taking the unconventional road requires a lot of persistence, some serious sacrifice, endless rejection, and a whole lot of hustle. It will push you to be more vulnerable, teach you how to think outside the box, and challenge you to boss up in big ways. So if you, too, have been wanting to quit your day job for a career filled with purpose, passion, and prosperity, then listen carefully, because here is how you can find your niche, build your empire, and get paid to do what you love!

Prioritize Play

If you want to get paid to play, it is important you make time for play. Although it might seem a little counterproductive, putting your passions on the top of your to-do list will help you get clear on the activities you actually enjoy doing. When I had my millennial meltdown and quit my steady job to focus more on life, my only priority was to do more of whatever made me happy. Studies show that play has the power to relieve stress, improve brain function, stimulate creativity, boost energy, and keep you feeling youthful. But thanks to the responsibilities that come with #adulting, playtime can be viewed as immature. Between a demanding work schedule and endless errands, it is easy to put your hobbies on the back burner, which, in turn, makes you lose sight of what really lights you up! So if you have forgotten how to play or are feeling a little lost while thinking to yourself, "What the heck is my passion?" give yourself permission to try new things and explore different ideas.

Maybe you want to take up a serious hobby such as running 5ks on the weekends, writing poetry, making jewelry, or painting glorious pictures of the sunset. It could be something as silly as roaming the aisles at Target, playing with puppies, or binge-watching "The Bachelor" every Monday. How you choose to spend your playtime doesn't matter. What matters is that you make a personal promise to do more of what makes you happy. Adding this kind of awareness into your fun will only help you discover your talents, ignite your imagination, and begin to fulfill your purpose.

Practice Makes Perfect

Anyone can become an expert with enough practice. However, a lot of us do not allow ourselves to start all over again because of the dedication, patience, and persistence it takes to master a craft. Some people take years to become specialists in their fields, while others are just born with natural talent. Regardless of where you stand in this scenario, let me tell you another sea-cret: You will never reach your full potential without practice because if you don't use it, you lose it. As you put in the work over and over again, it becomes second nature, helping you become more confident in your abilities.

As I began to explore my passion for writing, I decided to start a blog. Was it good? Of course not! I could barely spell, let alone form a functional sentence, but I did not let that stop me. I knew if I stuck with it, I was only going to get better. Every week, I wrote an article inspired by a workout I did, a recipe I made, or an encounter I experienced and shared it with my audience (and when I say audience, I really mean a handful of friends and my mother). Regardless of how many people were reading, or how skilled I thought it was, I made it a point to post every week. This kind of consistency transformed my writing from a hobby to a habit.

After years of practice, I was able to establish my voice, improve my storytelling ability, and believed it was possible for me to write a book. It is pretty cool to know these words you are holding in your hands at this moment would not be possible without the effort I put into my practice. If you plan to make a profit from your passions, then you have to put in the energy to sharpen your skillset. Whether you are already an accomplished musician or are trying to become the next "Top Chef." I encourage you to develop a regular practice regimen into your weekly calendar and work on taking your game to the next level.

Find Your Niche

Once you get clear on what your passions are and learn how to master your craft, then you can dig a little deeper and discover your niche. In the business world, a niche is what makes your brand unique, setting you apart from the crowd. When it comes to figuring out your niche, you should build from your expertise and try to think about where the competition is lacking.

For example, when I came up with my mermaid act, there was no shortage of street performers in Hawaii. However, I did notice those streets were missing a bit of island magic. I knew that tourists would go wild if they met a mermaid while vacationing in Hawaii, so I made it my mission to give the people what they wanted! And do you know how many visitors were thrilled to find a mermaid while strolling the streets? Enough to pay my rent . . . that's how many.

As you begin to build a business, it's easy to feel like a little fish in a big pond, or in this case, a little mermaid in a big ocean. There are so many routes you can go and various ways you can grow. Having a niche will help you hone in on one specific task rather than overwhelm you with endless possibilities. It provides a better understanding of the audience you are trying to reach and attracts you to the right community of customers. That way, you can make a lasting impact on the people you truly want to help.

When it comes to finding your niche, you have to get clear on what you have to offer. Let your quirks shine, embrace your silly side, and give others a peek into your brain. People want to feel inspired, but they also want to feel connected to you and your brand. Letting your walls down will not only help with your authenticity, but it will also help you recognize what makes you, YOU! Try not to think too hard about it, though, because your niche will come to you in time. Just start doing what feels right, and every so often, check in with what is working for you, research what your clientele wants, and believe there is a spark in you that sets you apart from the pack.

Dreams Don't Work Unless You Do

Shout out to anyone sitting on her rear end, waiting patiently for an opportunity to come knocking on her door. You are too cute. If you think good things come to those who wait, think again. Everyone knows that good things come to those who hustle.

To the outside eye, the opportunities I have received might seem as if I was in the right place at the right time, but that could not be further from the truth. What sets a lucky person apart from an unlucky person is her tenacity. These opportunities did not happen by spending my days daydreaming. As a matter of fact, they were a result of my hard work and hustle.

When it comes to creating opportunity for you and your brand, you have to be willing to put yourself out there. Send emails, pitch ideas, hit up networking conferences, make phone calls, exchange business cards, and let others know what you have to offer! This is the part of business that can be intimidating to most, but you will never get an opportunity if you don't ask for it. You have to keep your eyes peeled and your heart opened to the situations that matter. Do your best to be aware of the people surrounding you, look for ideas that match your interests, and believe that opportunity is around every corner. Then, when you are presented with your big break, make sure you are ready for it because part of creating opportunity is being prepared for when it strikes. For example, if you are dying for the chance to be on "The Bachelor" since Bachelor Monday is how you prefer to play, then as you wait for the opportunity to audition, it's time to start making moves. Go on dates to prepare yourself for those intimidating one-on-one's and get your body in the best shape of your life so you can stand your ground next to those pageant girls. Get clear on your intentions for wanting to be on the show and even go to the extreme of planning out a legendary limo exit. That way, when you finally come face to face with a casting director, you will be ready to shine with confidence! I know it might seem kind of crazy to make big moves with such a small chance of getting on the show, but if you really want it, this is how you work for it. Take initiative, create your own opportunities, and have the courage to really go for it!

Rejection is Just Redirection

As you get the hang of building your own doors of opportunity, you will also need to get comfortable with having them shut in your face. It sounds pretty harsh, I know, but I guess I'm just used to it. I have heard so many no's on my road to success that people actually refer to me as "The Queen of Rejection." While this title might be insulting to some, I wear it as a badge of honor because if you aren't getting rejected, you aren't trying. Being denied a dream fills us with feelings of failure, confusion, and personal doubt. This makes it a lot safer to sit in the shallow waters of certainty than to dive deep into the pain of disappointment. The energy that it takes to overcome this kind of mental upset is what keeps others living in the comfort zone rather than pursuing their passions. It is tough to take no for an answer. Not only do you have to find the strength to keep going, but you also have to find the faith to believe that something better is on the way. You have to remember how important it is to trust the process and applaud yourself for taking a chance. Whether you are applying for your dream job or asking someone out on a date, try to use every experience as a way to learn, grow and prepare yourself for the success that is meant for you!

Looking back on all the times people turned me down, I have a heart full of gratitude knowing that rejection made me resilient and more importantly, it led me to exactly where I am supposed to be. If I would have been hired any one of the six times I interviewed to be a flight attendant, was offered a hosting position for The Lakers after my audition, or became a famous beer blogger as I had planned, then I wouldn't have written this book. I wouldn't have had the chance to travel the world. And I sure as heck would not be the mermaid I am today!

Although rejection might seem like it is the end of the world, it is really just the beginning of a new realm of possibility. The next time you hear a "thanks, but no thanks," hang on to the hope that something better is around the corner.

Less Talking, More Doing

Anyone can talk about her goals, dreams, or entrepreneurial aspirations, but talk is cheap and we are trying to get paid, remember? Expressing all the success you wish to reach one day means nothing if you are refusing to take decisive action. What you do has a greater value than what you say you are going to do.

Don't get me wrong, I am not telling you to keep your dreams bottled up inside. I fully believe there is a special kind of magic that comes from sharing your ambitions with others. When you dream out loud you are being held accountable for your actions, as well as opening yourself up to people who just might be able to help make your dreams come true. But without action, your dreams will remain dreams, and no one will take you seriously when it comes time to make them happen. Can you imagine if I just sat around telling people I was a mermaid? No one in her right mind would believe me and honestly, how could I expect that? Mermaids only exist in folklore legends and Disney cartoons. But since I took initiative to become a mermaid entertainer, rather than just entertain the idea in my head, my friends, family, and community started to believe in this chosen path.

If you have always talked about starting your own online business or find yourself telling everyone about the podcast you are hoping to launch one day, then what in Poseidon's name are you waiting for? Follow through with these goals by purchasing a domain, investing in the equipment, designing a logo, and creating the content. You don't have to know the exact product you will sell on your website. And you sure as heck don't have to know what you will talk about on your podcast. All you need to do is keep taking small steps in the right direction, and trust that the results you can't stop talking about will happen. Actions speak louder than words, so instead of telling people what you are going to do, show 'em.

Collaboration Over Competition

I will be the first to admit, in college, I sucked at group projects. I either stressed myself out by doing too much of the work or was one of those partners that was always MIA (sorry, Hillary). I always thought group projects were pointless until I entered the "real world" and was able to see how much easier it is to reach success by working together.

Regardless of what you choose to pursue as your career, there is no need to go at it alone. Behind every great girlboss is a business bestie to hype her hustle and keep her Instagram pics on point. Thanks to modern-day marketing, seeking out a dependable partnership could be intimidating at first. It seems that everywhere you turn there are people who have more success, a better skill set, or more Instagram followers than Kendall Jenner. Do your best to steer clear of the comparison trap and instead spotlight what you have to offer. Whether you are building a brand or trying to grow within your company, don't feel threatened by other people who are slaying in your industry. Stay in your lane and turn your idea of competition into companionship. There is plenty of room for everyone to succeed. Rather than worrying about being better than a fellow contender, work together to create, promote, and celebrate each other's victories! Reach out to other women working hard to get their big break, and see if you can collaborate on a fun project. You don't have to go at it alone, there are people out there who need you to grow just as much as you need them!

Money is a Vibe

If you believe money is the root of all evil, allow me to shift your money mindset. The truth is, money is an energy source flowing to us freely. However, if you hold on to it with a white-knuckle grip and believe there is not enough to go around, then don't act surprised if it doesn't show up more in your life.

It is time to go inward and get super clear on your relationship with money. Does it bring stress and worry into your life? Are you too afraid to spend it? Or maybe you find yourself spending more than you have? Do you share it with people in need? Do you value every penny? What is your idea of financial freedom? Okay, okay, okay. Enough with the twenty-one questions. But to be honest, a lot of us are afraid to talk about money, let alone admit that we want to make a lot of it. We let it rule our lives, convinced we don't have enough money to do what we want or secure what we desire. However, when you begin to learn your worth, value your time, and believe that money is abundant, then you will understand the joy that comes from financial freedom.

As you can see, this part of the chapter is not about getting paid to play as much as it is about getting paid—period. Here is how you can tap into that cash flow and begin to manifest more sand dollars in your life:

+ **Pay It Forward**
  You get what you give, so if you have the money to spare, share it with a stranger. Surprise someone with a coffee, give a homeless person your spare change, and always, always, always, tip your bartenders.

+ **Appreciate Every Penny**
  If you don't learn how to be thankful for even the chummiest of change, why should you ever be gifted with more? My street performing days really taught me the value of a dollar. Anytime someone would slip some change into my bucket, I couldn't help but light up with joy. Showing appreciation toward every penny is how you show respect toward money, and when you respect money, you are rewarded with more.

+ **Use a #MoneyMantra**

If you want to call more money into your life, then start by saying it out loud! Y'all know how much I love my #MermaidMantras and creating an intentional focus on finance will only help improve your money mindset (and your bank account).

+ **Invest in Yourself**

They say you have to spend money to make money, and what better way to spend it than on your self! Put your money where your mouth is by investing cash toward your goals. It can be scary to spend your savings on the latest podcasting equipment or overpriced gym membership. But take it from a girl that dropped way too many sand dollars on a custom made mermaid tail—you can't put a price tag on happiness!

+ **Time Is Money**

It doesn't matter if we collect an hourly paycheck or annual salary; we get paid in exchange for our time. How do you choose to spend your time? Are you chipping away at your goals piece by piece, or are you avoiding them at all costs? Are you working for a company that utilizes your talents, or are you letting them waste away? If you find yourself complaining about not having enough hours in the day, try taking a step back to figure out how you can start making your time work for you!

+ **Believe You are Worthy**
  For the longest time, when people dropped big bills in my money bucket, I felt some guilt, as if I didn't deserve it. Why should anyone make money by dressing up as a mermaid? Eventually, I discovered that I am worthy of riches because I truly believe that I add value to this world. So when you are gifted financially for your efforts, accept it with grace, because you are well worth it!

My idea of financial freedom is not about having millions in the bank (although I am not against that). I believe financial freedom comes from building a healthy relationship with money. When you can spend it mindfully, look at it from a place of abundance, understand its true value, and use it for good, then how can it be the root of all evil?

Seek a Mentor

Setting out on a career path can be somewhat of a struggle, which is why finding a mentor is a must! Having an experienced ally show you the tricks of the trade will only help you grow both personally and professionally. Mentors are trusted advisors in whom you can confide whenever you begin to feel a little lost on your voyage to success. They can show you new skills—ones you may need to excel in the workplace—provide feedback to ensure you are reaching your fullest potential, and offer you the encouragement you covet to keep at it. These trusted leaders have already experienced the highs and lows of business, so why not learn from their mistakes and successes? Most mentors will share stories of when they first began and what they would've done differently if they could start all over again. Since they are already thriving in their businesses, mentors will help you get your foot in the door by introducing you to other leaders in the industry.

Now, how does one get connected with these career confidants? Bumble . . . just kidding. If only it were that easy. I mean, there are social apps that will connect you to like-minded hustlers, but just like dating, it still takes more effort than you may think. You have to show up to meetings, put yourself out there at networking events, sign up for seminars, and be willing to ask for help!

But if that kind of business vulnerability intimidates you, then look to the individuals who inspire you. Whose life do you watch with admiration thinking to yourself, "Hey, I can do that!" What is their story? How did they reach their level of success? Read about them, learn about them, study them, and I mean this in the least stalker-ish way, become obsessed with them. Buy tickets to their events, surround yourself with their energy, and research their interviews! They have already paved the way to a life you dream of living, so why not follow in their footsteps?

After making my move back to California, I wasn't really sure how to go about mermaid business on the mainland, so a friend connected me with someone who had her own entertainment company. After sharing my story with her, I was welcomed on as one of her performers, which took my mermaid game to the next level. I literally went from entertaining on the streets to flipping my fin at high-end hotels, community events, and even the occasional local news appearance. Not only did this woman welcome me into her pod with open arms, but she also became my "mermaid manager," booking me gigs and teaching me how to be the best dang mermaid I could be. My claim to fame is thanks to the guidance of Kim, and I am thankful to have learned from the best in the mermaid business. It doesn't matter if you are a college graduate unsure of your next move or a girl boss looking to quit your day job and become a mermaid. If you are feeling lost on your own journey, do not hesitate to ask a mentor for some direction. Open your mind up to the feedback, support, and guidance that others have to offer and allow them to help you reach new levels of success!

Fake It Till You Make It

As you set out on your career path, there will be moments when you feel like a fraud. Perhaps you are not the most qualified candidate for the job or have the idea you don't deserve any fame and fortune. You might think, "Who am I to start a business? What talents do I have to offer others? Why would they ever choose me to be on 'The Bachelor?'" But guess what? You are capable, deserving, and worthy of all the success you desire.

It takes a little time to get there, so be patient with the process. Stop becoming a victim of the imposter syndrome. This psychological sickness makes us feel inadequate while causing fear of being exposed as a fake in our work lives. Moments of self-doubt tend to stem from the societal expectations we put on each other and ourselves. But if you continue to wait around for the validation of others instead of owning up to your dreams, then you will never make it.

You owe it to yourself to become everything you have ever wanted, so stop doubting and start doing.

Faking it is not about making others buy into your vision of success; it's about believing in what you have to offer. There is nothing wrong with enhancing your resume to highlight your expertise or apply for a promotion despite the little experience you may have. Titles are for the entitled. Always remain true to your passions, talents, and overall happiness to find success within your life.

When I began my mermaid gig, I never thought it would lead me down the career path that it has become today. At the time, I was just looking to make people smile while adding a little bit of magic to the crowded streets of Hawaii. Rather than getting caught up in the money, I would make, the status it would bring, or the 401k benefits it might (or might not) provide, I found fulfillment in the play. You see, the real reward in this kind of business is bringing a sense of joy to others by inspiring them enough to believe. Everyone was able to see the mermaid in me because I was confident enough to see it in me. This unconventional career path fuels me with the sense of purpose that our soul-searching generation yearns for. The moment I decided to quit my day job and become a mermaid was the moment I discovered we all have something special to offer this world. It is up to you to go out there and hustle hard. Create opportunity, master your skillset, ask for help, tap into your creative genius, and trust in your talents. Your only job in this life is to share your unique gift with the world.

Then, as you begin to put in the work, sit back and enjoy as life begins to work for you.

Chapter 5

Fight the Funk

*I*n the whimsical world of Instagram, life as a mermaid is beaming with sunshine and rainbows. But don't let the filters fool you. Allow me to open your eyes to an unsaturated reality: Even mermaids have their gloomy days.

I have developed this positive persona in which people always expect me to be happy, and while it's flattering to be a person that others feel comfortable turning to for inspiration and guidance, I often feel like a fake, knowing there are days when I do not feel like my happiest and most fierce self.

The uncertainty of my future and my tendency to overthink life often leave a dark rain cloud of doubt lingering above me. It is almost as if I am drowning in the downpour of my dreams as the universe tests my faith and challenges my patience.

Now you might be thinking, "Gennah, this is a book about mermaids, happiness, and making the most of life. Why are you telling me about your deep-rooted issues?"

Because I know I am not alone in these feelings of funk.

We live in a society that expects us to be ecstatic with the thought of life, but let me be the first to tell you, "It is okay not to be okay." Sometimes life can be exhausting, and our days are filled with one big frustration after another—you lose your job, your car gets towed, you catch your boyfriend cheating, you get hit with food poisoning, you accidentally delete your research paper, or your car gets towed again. Trust me when I say, we have all been there (okay, so maybe not the boyfriend cheating thing, but I did get my car towed twice in the same week). But what if I told you all that was surface level stress, and the cause of unhappiness tends to go beyond the typical PMS symptoms and first-world woes?

Mental illnesses, such as depression and anxiety, are on the rise, and these physiological disorders are becoming more common within our modern generation. According to the World Health Organization, 300 million people around the world suffer from depression, and nearly fifty percent of all people diagnosed with depression are also battling anxiety issues. Although you may feel as if you are fighting this internal battle alone, chances are, the people around you are suffering in silence with you.

Do not let mental imbalance keep you from believing in the ability to experience your own bliss. Happiness begins in the mind. It comes from the reaction to your struggles, your perception toward unavoidable situations, and the ability to control your emotions. When you become more conscious of your #MOOD, you can navigate through the bad jujus and rekindle with the good ones.

Come on. We are living in the Kid Cudi era, so of course, everyone here is "on the pursuit of happiness." Our common aspiration is to "be happy" but what many of us don't understand is happiness is less about being and more about doing. You probably read somewhere that happiness is a choice, and I want to break down what that really means. Being blissed out is not as much of a choice as it is a result of our choices. Meaning, if you want to be happy, then you have to do more of the stuff that makes you happy! Whether you suffer from the dark side of depression or you struggle to get back up when life knocks you down, there are a number of ways to reset, re-center, and reconnect with your brightest self. Here is how to fight the funk on the kind of days where getting out of bed and taking a shower is the last thing you want to do.

Look Good, Feel Good

You thought I was kidding about the whole shower thing, but I figured what better way to start fighting the funk than by washing the funk off. Whether you opt for soaking in the tub, steaming it up in the shower, or going for a hippy dip in the ocean, all mermaids can probably agree that water has a way of cleansing the spirit, leaving you rejuvenated, refreshed, and revived.

After you have rinsed off the stank energy your funkiness caused, slip into your Sunday best and swipe on some bronzer to enhance that glow. Curl your eyelashes, rock some lipstick, and pencil in your eyebrows. Do whatever it is you have to do to put yourself together. Although it may sound vain, I fully believe putting effort toward your appearance triggers a sense of pride.

The way you care for yourself is a reflection of how much you care about yourself.

If you want to be a slob-ka-bob that avoids wearing real pants and cannot remember the last time you brushed your hair, I'm here to say, "Go for it!" The choice is yours, remember? Just don't be surprised when life starts feeling like one big hot mess. On the flip side, when you choose to clean up your act, I guarantee you will attract more beauty into your life. When you look good, you feel good, and when you feel good, you are drawing in more good energy.

Dance It Off

At this point in our friendship, I feel like you should know how much I live for my spontaneous dance parties. (If you have no idea what I am talking about, then please do yourself the favor and refer back to Chapter One.) Dancing is a style of movement therapy, which is often used to treat depression and anxiety. Your mind and body are intimately connected. Although your brain is the controller of your body's movement, the way you move can also affect the way you think and feel. Studies have shown that moving your body is a "two-way street," meaning motion in the body will help relieve you of stress in the mind, as well as dampen the anxiety building up within.

Moving and grooving instantly enhances your energy by stimulating endorphins and awakening the spirit hiding in your heart. Before you choose to become a victim of your wallflower ways, I want to stress the fact you do not have to be an all-star twerker or breathtaking ballerina to encounter the trance that dance has to offer. All you have to do to feel this kind of mental stimulation is simply move to the melody. Get out of your head, release any doubt, and focus more on the bodily sensations. This kind of practice enhances internal awareness by shedding light on how you feel at the moment. Allow your emotions to flow through the body rather than staying stuck in your mind.

When in Doubt, Cry It Out

Another way to reap the healing benefits of water is to allow yourself to ball your eyes out like a little beeyotch. Although crying has earned a reputation to be viewed as emotionally unstable, I will be the first to reassure you there is nothing wrong with letting the floodgates flow. And the uglier the cry, the better. Just look at Kim Kardashian. She might have all the money, resources, and husbands in the world, but the girl still ugly cries more than any celebrity should (and you can peep at the countless memes to prove it). Even though it does make for some juicy reality TV, I like to think the real reason for her meme-worthy meltdowns is because it frees her of the pain and drama that comes from being married to Kanye West.

Crying cleanses us mentally by releasing pain, stress, and toxins that we tend to bury and carry around with us. It is almost impossible not to feel a wave of relief after shedding some tears, even if our circumstances remain the same. Don't be ashamed of the mascara and snot running down your face. Just grab yourself a box of Kleenex, and let it all out.

Take a Digital Detox

While there is no doubt that technology has made life easier for us all, (thanks, Google) it's also one of the main reasons behind the rapid rise of depression and anxiety found in our society. We spend an average of five hours a day emailing, scrolling, liking, commenting, refreshing, scrolling some more, sharing, and watching one obnoxiously hilarious cat video after another. As a result of those dang, cute cat videos, we are less focused, less productive, and more out of tune with reality.

And don't even get me started on the constant comparison trap that we are all guilty of, myself included. We all know that social media is just a highlight reel of the good moments, so why do we get so worked up in comparing our lives to a complete stranger whom we follow on the Internet? I don't know about you, but this self-destructive habit only makes me feel jealous, inadequate, or even unsure of WTH I am actually doing with my own life.

- "Why don't I have X amount of followers?"
- "Why am I not getting free workout clothes from big-time brands?"
- "Why am I not traveling to Europe by yacht while sipping on rosé with a dude from France?"

By triggering these emotions of envy and resentment, the digital world, and social media in general, can make us feel like we are not enough. Which is why routine detoxes are crucial for your overall wellbeing. Taking a step back from the technology gives your brain a break from information overload and allows you to breathe again. Challenging yourself to a digital detox will give you time to think deeply, make better decisions, be productive, and connect with yourself and the people around you. If you are already breaking into a cold sweat and suffering from withdrawals at just the thought of powering down, then you, my friend, need it the most.

So how does one successfully complete a digital detox? I am glad you asked! Did you know there are actual retreats in desired travel destinations where the use of electronics is prohibited? If you don't have a week to escape from both the real and digital world, don't sweat it. There are plenty of other ways to keep your social media-obsessed self in check. Start by turning off your push notifications. That way, anytime you get a like on your latest Instagram selfie, you are not tempted to open the app and start scrolling.

Another reason our devices are so alluring is the vibrant screen instantly stimulates the mind. You can change the brightness in your settings, or even make it black and white. That way, you will not experience the same kind of feeling when unlocking your screen. Other ways to promote less phone time and more "me" time is keeping your bedroom a tech-free zone, putting your phone away at mealtime (yes, that means no #foodporn pics), and spring cleaning your social media accounts. Don't be afraid to unfollow the people who are not fueling your feed with positive, uplifting, and encouraging vibes. A 2018 study performed with students at the University of Pennsylvania showed the more time we spend on social media, the worse we feel. So if you get to the point where you doubt yourself, try quitting the app cold turkey and see how you feel.

Like anything in life, the first step to overcoming your addiction is to be aware. If you know that technology is the root of your unhappiness, disconnect from it all, and take the time you need to reconnect with your true self.

Look for the Lesson

Who says school is the only place you will be tested? There will always be a lesson to learn through every experience in life. And the most beneficial of lessons are usually the ones that make you want to pull your hair out.

Take, for example, the time my car got towed twice in one week. The first time it happened, I had parked it at my usual spot for work. Even though I should not have been parking there for the last year, I never let it stop me. As I pulled in with excitement to find such a prime spot with little time to spare, I noticed the tiniest voice in my head, asking me a valid question. "Will today be the day when I actually get towed?"

"Never," I thought and headed into work without a worry in the world. Six hours later, I wandered back out into the parking lot with my beautiful Luna girl nowhere to be found (and yes, I am one of those people who names her car). If you have ever had your car towed, you know how the rest of this story goes; head to the tow yard, identify the car, show proof of ownership, pay way too much money for bail, and finally head home. The lesson? Do not park there anymore! Unless you are just heading into the gym for a quick sweat sesh, of course, because that is exactly what I did later that very same week. Could I have parked down in the structure and had my parking validated by the gym? Yes. But did I? No. Because I was in such a rush, I didn't want to put in the time, let alone make the effort to drive down, get my ticket, walk up the stairs, and across the shopping center, all while remembering to get my ticket validated later. So I just parked in a place I was not supposed to and, again, my Luna girl got taken away from me.

I was trying to take a shortcut, and as a result, the universe taught me a major lesson in slowing down and tuning into what my intuition was trying to tell me. This was an expensive lesson to learn, but now I know that I need to stop jam-packing my schedule to the point where I am too busy to stop, breathe, and listen to my own thoughts.

So the next burden you face in life, shift your perspective from, *why is this happening to me?* To, *what is this situation teaching me?*

Talk it Out

I get it. No one likes a "Debbie downer," but sometimes talking out your problems and simply venting to someone who is willing to listen will help free you from whatever negative emotions you may be experiencing. Lucky for us, therapy is becoming less of a taboo and more of a tradition in today's age of anxiety.

During therapy, a well-trained counselor or therapist will listen to your problems and help you find your own answers, without any judgment. A therapist will also give you time to talk, cry, shout, or simply think. It is an opportunity to look at your problems in a different way with someone who will respect you and your opinions. Since you will be opening up about situations that you might not feel comfortable sharing with anyone else, it is important you do the research and find a therapist that is right for you.

And if you do not feel comfortable talking to a therapist, or feel as if there is no one to turn to who will understand, then I suggest going inward and try communicating with yourself through a juicy journaling session. Taking the time to put your thoughts on paper will slow you down and allow yourself to listen to what your heart is trying to say. As a matter of fact, I recommend journaling out your feelings before talking to someone about them. It will clear your mind while helping you discover the root of your dilemma. Whatever it is you are going through, it is important to know that you are not alone. There are others out there dealing with the same issues and waiting for someone to be vulnerable enough to share their feelings with. Open up, let it out, and share some of the weight you are carrying on your shoulders with your family, friends, community, or anyone else willing to listen. We are all here for you, sea sister!

Burn Baby Burn

Thanks to its captivating light, crackling noises, and cozy warmth, fire brings out the pyro in all of us. The mesmerizing flame seems to have healing powers to relax the body, calm the mind, and soothe the spirit. You can reap the benefits from the privacy of your home or under the magic of a starry night. These are my favorite ways to ignite the inferno and use fire to fight off the funk.

+ **Indulge in Aromatherapy**
  Candles instantly spark a sense of relaxation. Their subtle scents have been proven to ease tension, increase self-awareness, and promote a peaceful feeling. Some cultures stare into the flickering flame of a candle as a form of meditation, while other people tend to bring them along for a bubble bath. Even Brittney Spears has been known to use candles in her gym, at least until she burned it down. However you decide to use candles, just be smart and blow them out before you leave the room!

+ **Have a Smudge Party**
  In the spiritual world, sage, palo santo, and even incense carry the magic to cleanse your energy. Whether it is conflict at work or a stressed-out partner bringing you down at home, using these spiritual sticks encourages you to approach

things with an unburdened mind. This kind of aura clearing will rid you of any negativity you are carrying around while making space for new energy to enter.

+ **Spark Up Your Thoughts**

Our mind is easily overwhelmed with negative thoughts and irrational fears, which can easily lead to feelings of funk. Try writing any unnecessary thoughts down on a piece of paper to burn. Then watch any doubts disappear, as the flames slowly swallow your worries, making them vanish into thin air, a smoke signal to The Universe.

+ **Get Lit**

I know smoking seaweed might not be every mermaid's favorite pastime, but since I was born on 4/20, I like to think the ganja is in my blood. Hitting the reefer always calms my mind, gets my creative juices flowing, and takes my spirit a little . . . uh, higher. With the legalization of cannabis on the rise, weed is becoming widely accepted and highly recommended by society. Weed does have a reputation of turning you into a space cake or causing you to move slower than a sloth, but if used under the right circumstances, it also has the ability to magnify your focus, ignite your imagination, and even heal your hangover!

Don't get me wrong, I am not trying to peer pressure you into becoming a pothead. And if it's not legal where you are, I'm not telling to become a criminal or dish out peer pressure like a cool kid in high school. I am just saying, don't knock it until you try it. If you have trouble sleeping, deal with joint pain, or find yourself feeling anxious, then take a hit and chill the F out. One tiny toke is more than enough to soothe the soul. How you choose to take your dosage of chill is up to you, just be sure to use it responsibly and always be mindful of your munchies.

Never Miss a Sunset

You know what you should have, could have, would have done differently to have a better day, but at the end of it all, there is nothing you can really do except let it go. Sunsets have the magical power to add a spark of wonder and awe into your day-to-day life by bringing more peace and presence to your surroundings. Taking a time-out to soak up the magical beauty of a golden hour is a glorious way to reflect on the day you just experienced while believing in the possibility of tomorrow. It's the ultimate way to reset your mood and reboot your bliss because every time you witness the setting sun, you are reminded it will also rise again. So the next time you sense the feeling of darkness in your heart, make a date with the sunset and trust that you will find your light again.

Take a Catnap

One of my old roommates was (and probably still is) the catnap queen. I swear, sometimes before I even woke up to begin my day, the girl had already taken three power naps. But it makes sense since she is one of the happiest people I know. Being tired can make you more uptight, stressed, and impatient with others. According to a 2019 study from the University of California, Berkeley, Senior Sleep Researcher Matthew Walker found when people don't get enough sleep, they show significantly more activity in areas of the brain that are associated with anxiety. However, for some odd reason, napping is often frowned upon in our workaholic culture. Many believe napping is for the lazy and unambitious. Anyone who falls asleep at her desk during work or school is constantly laughed at, and even when we doze off, we have a tendency to feel a little guilty. But don't let the nap-shamers keep you from a mid-day slumber.

Naps can be one of the most powerful tools for self-improvement; they can increase not only our health and wellbeing but our intelligence and productivity, as well. On those days where you are not feeling upbeat, energized, and motivated to take on the day, allow yourself to catch up on some Zs with a power nap. Taking a time-out for some shut-eye is the perfect reset button for your day. It is a great way to wake up feeling rejuvenated and refreshed while improving your alertness and overall performance. Just be sure to keep naptime to twenty to thirty minutes. As I mentioned before, slipping into a full-on REM cycle can do more harm than good.

Breathe Through the Bitterness

When the overwhelming whirlwind of life begins to suffocate you with stress, calm yourself down, and just breathe. Our emotions have a way of building up in the body, and we store them as tension. Our shoulders, hips, even jaw and forehead all flare up with feelings. When this kind of resistance happens in the body, it is urgent that you release the emotional agony through your breath.

I notice a major shift in my behavior on the days I skip meditation compared to the days where I get my "om" on first thing in the morning. I am impatient, short-tempered, tired, breathless, and just a straight-up sea wench to the people around me. I typically blame PMS, but in my heart, I know I can only blame myself. These temperamental mood swings are because I don't allow myself to sit in stillness, connect with my breath, and fuel my mind with good thoughts for the day. I can write an entire book on the magic of meditation, but for now, know that anytime you find yourself overly anxious, all you have to do is inhale the good, empowering air and exhale the negative stuff.

Focus on the Good

Challenging your mind to focus on all that is going right in your life, rather than all that is going wrong, helps train your brain to accept the good with the bad. I know, it is tough to shift your mindset this kind of way, especially if you just got your fourth speeding ticket or are feeling anxious at the thought of running into your ex with his new fiancé. It is in our nature to fixate on the bad experiences and emotions that come into our lives, but this pattern of thinking is what pulls us deeper and deeper into the dreariness of depression.

Negative encounters tend to leave stronger impressions than positive ones because they trigger more intense reactions. As a result, we develop a selective memory for failures and setbacks—which can cause us to feel helpless or victimized or perhaps shy away from opportunities of joy. But no mermaid is a victim. We are our own heroes because of the way we chose to perceive and create our realities through mindful actions. Even during the times when life punches you in the gut, there is still so much to be thankful for.

Take a timeout and recognize all the good fortune surrounding you at this moment. Chances are you have a place to lay your head, a beating heart, people who love you, and enough money in the bank to treat yo'self to this entertaining read. What else can you think of at this moment that has the power to bring a smile to your face and appreciation to your heart? Write it down and revisit it on those days when you struggle to shake the sadness.

Embrace the Bad

The obstacles we face are not meant to punish us; they are put on our path to help us grow stronger and more confident in ourselves. It is the norm to feel fed up, overwhelmed, and stressed out with life, but the important part is to make sure you never give up on yourself. Without the bad, it would be harder for us to not only recognize, but also appreciate the good. So any funk you might be fighting right now, welcome it with open arms. Give yourself time to heal and trust in your ability to overcome the pain. You might not be able to knock out the funk like Mike Tyson, but now you have the tools to put up one heck of a fight. The reality is, happiness is a mind game. Stuff happens and everyone experiences unfortunate circumstances, but it is how you choose to perceive these situations that separate the happy from the unhappy. Challenge your mind to discover beauty in the darkness, put forth the work to do more of the stuff that brings you joy, and have faith you will soon find your light again.

Chapter 6

Become Cycle Sisters
With The Universe

Once upon a time, when I began to experiment with the concept of spirituality, I found myself making a conscious effort to connect with what others called, "The Universe." Although I couldn't quite see it yet, I did believe in it and started to do everything in my power to join forces with this mysterious energy.

For a month, I began meditating, appreciating, and trusting in its power. Then one evening, I received an unexpected visit from "Aunt Flo." This typical (and annoying) time of the month didn't really phase me until I caught a glimpse of the full moon that night, colored with a dark red hue. That's right. Because of my faithful dedication to this spiritual practice, I began my period the same night as the infamous "Blood Moon" eclipse that took place in 2014. While others would consider this a mere coincidence, there is no denying that I connected so intimately with the cosmos, we synced up and became full on cycle sisters like a sorority house during rush week.

It was the first time I saw The Universe in all of her glory, and now, I make it a point to slow down and admire its spellbinding spirit all around me. I see it in the sway of the trees, I hear it in the roar of the ocean, and I feel it in the power of my breath.

But maybe you don't believe in this high-vibin', good juju, universe-loving kind of spirituality, and that is totally okay. It doesn't matter if you believe in The Holy Spirit, Poseidon, or even eight-pound, six-ounce, sweet baby Jesus. Whatever you choose to believe in is not important. What is important is that you develop an awareness of and establish a relationship with this higher power. Because the truth is that there is a life far beyond your personal self.

But do not let that vast energy intimidate you. Although its power is so much greater than our own existence, its magic is within us all, and once you start to believe in it while learning how to tap into it, you will discover the ability to turn your wildest dream into a full-blown reality.

Have you ever heard of The Law of Attraction? This thought philosophy is among the most popular of the Universal Laws and is the belief that by focusing on positive or negative thoughts, we can bring positive or negative experiences into our lives. Meaning, if you wake up with the mindset that today is going to be a rough one, do not act surprised when you get a speeding ticket, shatter the screen of your brand new phone, or get ghosted by the dude you were dating. Whether you realize it or not, the energy you are cultivating within is what creates your outward reality. When we become victims to pessimistic thoughts of stress, jealousy, doubt, worry, and fear, we begin to vibrate at a lower frequency, bringing more stress, jealousy, doubt, worry, and fear into the world (go figure). So if you wish to experience more marvelous moments in your everyday life, it is necessary that you raise your frequency to attract those kinds of memorable encounters.

Since it is something that cannot be seen, this "frequency" that I speak about might be hard to wrap your head around, but think of it as a cell phone connection. It can be a bit confusing with all the 4G and LTE stuff, yet at its most basic form, the cell phone is a two-way radio consisting of a transmitter and a receiver that work together through of a special kind of energy wave. Now, I am no Steve Jobs, and to be honest, I don't know much about the wireless world. Nevertheless, I do know this: If your cell phone is not in range of these special signals, calls keep dropping, your Instagram feed refuses to refresh, and Google maps will start loading directions two exits too late. When your cell phone signal is low, even the latest version of the iPhone will start running like a first generation iPod. The same goes for your connection to the "special signal" around you. The Universe is like the transmitter radio, making you, my friend, the receiver. Together your frequencies are working to create a special energetic connection that keeps life performing at its best!

This way of thinking is a lot easier said than done. To truly raise our frequency to a 5G status, we have to full-heartedly believe that all we desire is possible, and put in the effort to keep our frequency vibing high. The keyword here being *effort*. As much as we would love to sit by the pool and work on our mermaid glow while the universe takes care of the rest—I hate to break it to you, but—that is not the way it works, sea sister. Since we are co-creating our reality with the energy surrounding us, we need to put forth actual effort for The Universe to gift us with VIP passes to Coachella or our own TV show on the Travel Channel. It first needs to see how hard you are willing to work.

I know I might sound a little crazy here (and by crazy, I mean full on psycho) but trust me on this one. The Universe is the real deal, and the sooner you learn how to connect with it, work with it, and believe in it, the sooner life will start to make sense.

Well . . . kind of.

Because even when you have a clear understanding of how it works, chances are, you will experience those moments of unexplainable magic where you find yourself asking, "How is this even possible?"

Here are some different ways you can take inspired action, raise your frequency, and connect so hard that you "sync up" with The Universe.

Get Your "Om" On

The inner peace that comes with shutting off the mind and focusing on your breath makes meditation a real no-brainer. This spiritual practice has a way of helping you tap into the intuitive guidance needed to co-create with The Universe. Taking the time to simply be connects you with the vibrational energy in the air, and gives you a moment to envision your deepest desires. But can someone please tell me why is it such a struggle to welcome this beneficial practice into our daily grind? In recent years, it has become an accepted fact that including meditation into your everyday life increases happiness, reduces stress, improves concentration, and even slows down the process of aging. It has the power to connect us with the present, while opening our minds to receiving unlimited information and ideas (i.e. from The Universe). So yeah, I think it is safe to say meditation is pure magic.

However, I personally understand how hard it can be to get in the groove of this major lifestyle change. Whether you have trouble slowing down your anxious brain or feel like there is not enough time in your jam-packed day, I am here to help you jump on the meditation bandwagon, so you too can reap the mind-blowing benefits. Here are some simple ways to begin cultivating your own meditation practice.

+ **Start Small**

    All it takes is three to five minutes of practice regularly to notice a major shift in your life. Over time your mind, body, and spirit will crave it. I recommend getting your "om" on first thing in the morning, to begin your day feeling centered and grounded, ready to make the most of your precious time.

+ **Get Outside**

    The best way to begin your meditation practice is to get outside and connect with the energy around you. Focus on the wind dancing through your hair, tune into the birds chirping cheerfully, imagine the warmth of the sun pouring into your heart, and breathe in all the beauty of that very moment. Sitting in stillness opens your senses to the energy of a higher power, and if you take the time to connect with that every day, it will stay within throughout your life journey.

+ **Find Guidance**

    If you are having a hard time zoning out, I recommend using a guided meditation. I like to think of it as training wheels for your practice, and then as you begin to feel more comfortable in your new habit, you can ditch the soundtrack and get to "om-ing" on your own. There are countless apps and downloadable series to lead you into oblivion. Some of my favorites include, Headspace, Calm, and Smiling Minds.

+ **Create a #MermaidMantra**
The hardest part of meditation is shutting off your mind. However, by focusing on a personal mantra, you will be able to get a better grasp of your thoughts and channel your energy to believing in your words. Find an affirmation, quote, or word that you wish to live up to, and make that the only idea floating in your head during your meditation session.

It is important to disconnect from the constant distraction surrounding us and focus on connecting to the power within. If you want to raise your vibration, I recommend beginning your meditation practice ASAP, but let us not forget—it is a practice. Some days will put you in the zone, while others will leave you feeling restless. If you continue to show up every day while having patience with yourself, the magic will follow.

Manifest Like a Mermaid

Before I teach you how to manifest like a mermaid, it is important that you develop a clear understanding of what manifesting actually is. In my opinion, it is a word that tends to get thrown around by a lot of people, but very few have a deep understanding of the actual meaning. Manifesting is believing something into its truth. It is knowing in your heart, one hundred percent, that what you may not be able to see yet is waiting for you to experience when the timing is *just* right. Maybe you already knew this, you little spiritual hotshot, you! But what you may not know is that manifesting the mermaid way takes a little more effort than crafting up a vision board, sticking Post-it notes of positive affirmations around the house, and waiting patiently for The Universe to make it all come true.

Manifesting like a mermaid requires fierce action, determined persistence, and continuous faith toward whatever your deepest desires may be. Hypothetically speaking, let's say it is brunching with Oprah. Well, a good way to manifest bottomless mimosas with Miss Super Soul herself is to start by getting clear on where you two would get together. Then, put in the continual effort by booking a reservation for two every month and show up to this dream date no matter how insane it feels—bonus points if you have enough guts to make the reservation under Oprah's name. As you start throwing back the bubbly at brunch, envision what you would talk about, ask yourself why you want to experience this moment, and believe with all of your heart that in time, Oprah will show up to this Sunday Funday and bring her bestie, Gayle, along for the celebration. You know what? Now that I am thinking about it, you might want to make that reservation for three.

New Moon, New Me

The moon is so freaking powerful. I often forget its compelling energy is what controls the oceans' tides. So as mermaids, obviously the good grace of our moon carries some kind of control over our spiritual selves! The average moon cycle lasts twenty-eight days, which is why it is incredibly ironic that I happened to start my own menstrual cycle the same day as the lunar phenomenon called the "Blood Moon." Since my cycle sister incident, I have been tapping into the energy of the moon every month by focusing on the qualities I wish to improve in myself, as well as what I need to let go of to grow.

This kind of self-reflection often takes place during the first phase of the new moon cycle. As I see that first sliver of the crescent moon, I take it one day at a time until the moon grows full. Now, this is where it can get a little challenging because patience is killer. But anytime you find yourself admiring the beauty of our glowing moon, reconnect with your "New Moon, New Me" intentions. Really put forth the effort toward living these intentions into truth and when the moon comes around full circle, step into your power by letting the new version of you to shine!

Spot the Synchronicities

The Universe speaks to us through coincidence. Think about it: Has an old friend ever crossed your mind, only for you to receive a phone call or text message from that exact same person no less than five minutes later? Or maybe one time, you had a strong desire to spend the weekend on a boat, and sure enough, you make friends with someone at your Saturday morning yoga class who—would you look at that—owns a boat. The next thing you know, she is inviting you onboard for a sunset sail, and you find yourself having a dance party on the poop deck wondering, "What is life?"

While many might believe it to be "luck" or "chance," it is really The Universe trying to show itself to you. When we become open, trusting, and present then synchronicity begins to pop up all over the place. By using this special kind of coincidence for guidance and validation, our lives become a dance with Universal energy, and our days begin to carry more meaning. Outside events start to align with our internal thoughts as The Universe leaves us a trail of breadcrumbs to follow toward all that we desire. The secret to spotting synchronicity is remaining present. It is more likely to occur when we have fully emerged ourselves in the moment and become more aware of our surroundings. So slow down, tune in, and smile at The Universe the next time you find yourself shaking it out on the poop deck.

Cultivate an Attitude of Gratitude

When we experience a life of gratitude, we recognize the endless love and constant support of the higher power while raising our frequency to the next level of consciousness. The art of appreciation helps lift your spirits and shift your mood resulting in a higher vibe (and by now, you should know what happens when your vibe is high). This spiritual practice carries the rare ability to slow down the speed of time, allowing us to fully connect with the present moment. It turns what we have into enough, while simultaneously providing us with even more—more energy, more patience, more compassion, and more all-around joy. As Jen Sincerio, author of *You Are a Badass*, so boldly states, "Gratitude is the gateway drug to awesomeness." To help you get high off the euphoria of life, here are different ways for you to get your gratitude fix:

+ **Keep a Gratitude Journal**

  This is probably the most effective strategy for increasing your level of gratitude. Keeping track of all the awe-inspiring moments you have to be thankful for allows you to create a sense of meaning in your life. End each day by giving thanks to the memorable moments of your day, and that way you can go back and reconnect with those thankful feelings later on in life.

+ ***Begin the Day with a Grateful Heart***

   Grant yourself an extra five minutes to revel in the comfort of your cozy bed and breathe in deep as you ponder all you have to be thankful for. Then, as you set out on your new day of possibility, focus on showing your appreciation toward those elements of prosperity every way you can. Just don't be so thankful for your bed that you slip back into a peaceful slumber and wake up feeling a little more resentful than grateful (yes, I am talking from experience here).

+ **Discover the Gift of Each New Day**

   The Universe rewards people who live in the now. Cue the term "present"—that is our ultimate gift in life. By slowing down and truly connecting with the moment, you will begin to discover the gifts hidden within each new day. It could be something as surprising as finding a $100 bill on the ground, or something as simple as a thumbs up from a kind stranger. Basically, it is any moment in time that brings a smile to your face and knowing you will remember it forever. When you begin to view life as a beautiful gift, you will be gifted in life.

+ **Write a Thank You Letter**

    In today's technology-driven society, receiving a hand-written letter in the mail holds more meaning now than ever before. Make someone's day by taking the time to write a letter expressing how thankful you are to have them in your life. Our relationships with others are the greatest sources of happiness. So as we build our gratitude practice, make it a primary focus to show appreciation toward the people who love you, support you, and believe in you.

+ **Rejoice in Life's Tiny Treasures**

    It could be a warm cup of coffee in the morning, spotting a beautiful butterfly, or maybe a steamy shower before you slip into a bed of fresh sheets. Whatever your vice may be, we can all agree it is the little things that bring us the most joy. Always remember to be grateful for life's tiny treasures by taking an innovative approach to appreciate the everyday luxuries that others may not be as fortunate to have.

Live To Give

Kindness makes the world go round, and to receive the abundance of love The Universe has to offer, you must give that same kind of compassion toward the world around you. Playing by the "Golden Rule" is a win-win for all parties. Not only does it have the power to fill you with a feeling of pride by acting kindly toward others, but it also has the potential to trigger bliss in those around you and inspire others to give what they can. Kindness is an epidemic and once you get bit by the bug, you will find yourself sharing, helping, and giving any way you can. The best part? It doesn't have to cost a dang thing! Here are a number of ways you can sprinkle some kindness into the lives of others and your own.

- Share a smile with a stranger.
- Help out a friend in need.
- Give a listening ear.
- Wrap someone in a warm hug.
- Cook dinner for someone special.
- Give your honest advice.
- Make someone's day by giving him or her a compliment.
- Send a motivating text to a friend.
- Give your time to someone.
- Write a heartfelt letter and mail it.
- Pick up the phone and give someone a call.
- Give someone a good laugh.
- Give forgiveness to a person you have been holding a grudge with.
- Clean out your closet and donate your clothes to a shelter.

Find Your Magic Minute

Is there a specific time where you always find yourself looking at the clock—11:11, 8:08, 1:23? While others may believe it to be the perfect time to make a wish, mermaids know to take that moment in time and simply be present. Your magic minute should be used as a reminder that you are on the right path and a confirmation that your actions are aligned with your purpose. However, if you don't feel that you are voyaging down the right path, use those sacred seconds to send a prayer asking for guidance. It is okay to feel lost, and it is okay to ask for help. As a matter of fact, The Universe wants to help, so don't hesitate to request a sign pointing you in the right direction. Your magic minute is the perfect time; it is in those sacred seconds that you are connected with the cosmos. This is a time to pay attention, be aware, stay grounded, and keep an open heart to whatever clue The Universe sends your way.

Call on Your Spirit Guides

Do you know who is one of the most underrated Disney characters around town? Dante, the kooky looking dog in the 2017 feature flick, *Coco*. If you are a loyal Disney+ subscriber like me, then you know which key character I am talking about. If not, then I will spare you the $6.99 a month and spill the beans. Although at first he seems like a silly stray dog that tags along with Miguel to the land of the dead, he is actually a spirit guide there to serve and protect him from harm. Whether it is your guardian angel, lost loved one, or a friend from the past, you are constantly surrounded by spiritual guidance. These mystic beings are here to offer us assistance and enhance our lives. It might sound a kind of kookoo at first, but surrendering to the idea that there are spirits looking out and supporting your every move allows you to carry yourself with unshakeable strength and undeniable faith. They are a trusted confidant, motivational cheerleader, and reliable BFF all wrapped into one. Like any relationship, it is necessary to build a connection based off of solid communication and intuitive trust. Here are ways to join forces with your spirit guides and get in tune with the metaphysical world:

+ **Ask for Help**

    Spirit guides will only work their magic when called upon. You have to ask for help regardless of how insane or uncomfortable it might feel. Requesting for their guidance doesn't have to be for help in these major and monumental moments, keep it small while you take the time to get better acquainted. Ask your guide to join you for a run, and then watch as you log a new personal record. You can also try inviting them on your morning commute to work. Just don't be surprised when you manage to catch every green light. As you begin to notice how dependable this invisible companion is, you will feel more sincere asking for the guidance and direction you desire.

+ **Be on the Lookout**

    If you want to receive the wisdom that your spirit guide has to offer, then you must be aware of the signs they are sending. It could be through music, through numbers, or even through the people you encounter during the day. Part of connecting with your divine guidance is slowing down your go-go-go mentality and opening up to the omens surrounding you.

+ **Tune Into Your Dreams**

    Dreaming is a legit way to connect with your spirit guides and follow internal insight. Dreams are basically stories and images that our subconscious minds create while we sleep. The dream world offers us insight into and inspiration for situations we are dealing with in the real world. And because our spirit guides are with us at all times, they are also able to reach out while we sleep. Take note of your dreams in the morning when they are fresh in your mind, and then use books, articles and Google as a resource to look up their underlying meaning.

+ **Put the Pen to Paper**

Neale Donald Walsch's bestselling book, *Conversations With God*, is the actual dialog between him and his powerful spirit guide. Granted, his spirit guide was Mr. G himself, but this book is a prime example of how communication with a higher existence can flow freely through us. The impressive part of this transformational story is the fun fact that it was written with only a pen, yellow legal pad of paper, and the honest questions in his heart. Our spirit guides are not only around us but also within us. Speaking to your spirit guides through free writing can give you answers to the truths you are seeking, while shining more light on your intuitive powers.

+ **Having Trust is a Must**

Having a spirit guide is like having an invisible friend all over again. Just because you can't see them, it doesn't mean they are not there for you. And although it might seem strange talking to thin air or referring to them by name, the only way this unseen connection will blossom is when you believe they are there listening, supporting, and loving you every step of the way. Trust is the key aspect to any relationship, including the sacred connection with your guides. Having trust will not only make you feel secure, it will also help you loosen up the rains a bit and let your guides work their magic! No one likes a crazy, controlling partner, not even spirit guides. Don't question them or doubt them, instead give them space to do their thing and trust in the unconditional love you have for each other.

Breathe in the Moment

Breathing is an orgasm of the soul. Am I right? Think of how many moans and groans you hear during a routine yoga class. It is because everyone in the room is getting off on their own breath. Nothing feels better than a big, deep, juicy breath. It helps to release all the resistance built up within the body, bringing more peace and harmony to the heart. Conscious breathing is an effortless way to raise your frequency and connect to the Universal energy within you. Imagine with every inhalation, you are breathing in all the beautiful energy surrounding you, and with each exhalation, focus on putting that same kind of beauty back out into the world. We've been breathing since we were born, so it might seem like second nature, but chances are you don't know how to breathe correctly. Pause for a second and take a deep inhale; notice from where you are breathing. Are you stuck in your chest? Or are you digging deep into your belly?

Many of us tend to breathe through our chest while building tension, stress, and anxiety, making it harder to physically catch our breath. But when we breathe from the belly, we can release all the resistance within ourselves, resulting in a calmer, cooler, and more collected state of mind.

I also use my breath for intuitive guidance. When I am troubled by a situation or unsure of a decision, I pause and listen to my breath. If it is short and shallow, then chances are I need to take a step back and rethink the circumstances. If it is deep, juicy, and makes me feel good, I simply trust that all will be well. Quiet the mind. Tune into the body. And start getting off on your own breath.

Let It Go, Let It Flow

Now I don't know about you, but I often find myself planning for the future. The reality is that the future is far beyond my control. Every time I set a goal, my mind slips into expectation mode, and I start obsessing over exactly how I wish it to play out. But where is the magic in that?

The thrill about co-creating your reality is letting go of expectations and trusting that your journey is unfolding exactly as it should. Waving your white flag and surrendering to the flow of life requires you to put full faith in the higher power, by believing every experience that happens to you is for your best benefit. Whether it is to teach you a lesson, give you a sign, or help you believe.

The Universe will always have your back.

I get it, though. We all experience trust issues, which is why we have a hard time loosening our grip. We get so frustrated when things don't go our way, and we come up with this wild idea that someone actually has it out for us. However, when we begin to build a trusting bond with The Universe, we will recognize that it is not trying to hurt us. As a matter of fact, this mysterious energy is guiding us and protecting us from experiencing a life that is not meant for us.

It's kind of like when your dog sees you eating chocolate and will not stop looking at you with those begging eyes filled with hope. You want to be the world's best dog mom and share some of the sweetness with your precious pup, but you know it will only lead to an expensive visit to the vet or possibly a one-way ticket to doggy heaven. Because you have your dog's best interest at heart, you don't even think twice about giving her even a lick of chocolate. Although your dog doesn't understand why she can't have any and will never know why you refused to give in to what she wants, your dog still chooses to love you. This is the same kind of loving connection you need to have with the higher power.

Although you might wish for a certain experience to unfold in your life, it is important to trust that if it is supposed to happen, it will. There is no need to look up to the higher power with begging eyes, hoping it will give you a taste of whatever it is you want. Instead, challenge yourself to let go of premeditated plans, fearful tendencies, and the urge to control. Focus on what you can do in each moment to raise your vibration, deepen your trust, and remain connected to the energy surrounding you. Believe that your higher power loves you enough to have the ultimate journey mapped out for you, and allow yourself to just go with the flow of life.

As you begin to build your bond with The Universe, remember to be patient. Like any relationship, it takes time while both parties work to create a foundation of trust. But as you incorporate these spiritual methods of meditation, gratitude, and manifesting into your daily life, you will start to experience the magic of Universal energy through synchronicity, opportunity, and breath. You will notice all these wonderful experiences unfolding around you, and one day you will trust The Universe so much, you would be able to ask her for a tampon if you needed to.

And of course, she would find a way to make one show up in your life because you are cycle sisters, and cycle sisters always have each other's backs.

Chapter 7

This Is Your Time, LIVE.

$\mathscr{G}$et ready to dive deep into the dark waters of your soul with this uneasy question.

If today were the day you took your last breath of life, would you be happy with the legacy you leave behind?

I know "the end" can be a touchy subject for most, but ironically, it's the one experience we collectively share. Not even mermaids are immortal. Our journeys will eventually reach the destination of death, and I am curious to know how that makes you feel? Are you out there trying to make the most of this minuscule amount of time you have? Or are you one of the many that choose to ignore this twisted reality, saving all your marbles for that "one day?" Because if that is the case, chances are you haven't had an encounter with the grim reaper yet.

I hate to be the bearer of bad news, but one day you will get hit with a major wake-up call, whether you lose someone dear to your heart or you come close to the kiss of death yourself. As tough as this reality is to swallow, it is not meant to worry you. These rude awakenings are here to shake things up and remind us how fortunate we truly are to be gifted with this one precious life. Dealing with loss is hard, but there is always a lesson to be learned. I received my first wake-up call when I lost a friend who had filled the world with so much light. His name was Sean Moses.

Mr. Moses had an alluring presence and a smile as radiant as his passion for life. You could feel the warmth in his heart and see the fire in his eyes. He was an actor, photographer, teacher, coach, writer, philosopher, and masseuse. One second he was living out of his car, the next he was balling alongside Will Ferrell in Tropic Thunder. He had the courage to pursue any and every dream his heart desired without any pressure of success. He was a world traveler with the kind of charisma that turned strangers into family. He always captured the attention of an eager audience through his entertaining stories, but he never allowed it to outshine his ability to listen. Helping others overcome obstacles and achieve their personal goals was his true talent. Since his positive spirit and remarkable energy was always in high demand, he utilized Facebook as a way to encourage and connect with his friends from all over the world. Each new day, he shared a quote that challenged our minds and opened our eyes to new perspectives of life. And for the record, this was back in 2012, before motivational quotes were the cool thing to do. (Did I mention he was also a trendsetter?)

On his final day, he shared a photo with this empowering quote.

Your life is now, seize it and make it amazing. Find your voice, discover your passion and pursue it. Be honest, generous and kind. Surround yourself with love, laughter and truth. Let your heart be your guide. Make a difference. Be brave and wild at heart. Take chances; be fearless. This is your time.

He captioned it with one word and one word only: "**LIVE.**"

Now that is one heck of a last word, but as you can see, Mr. Moses was one heck of a guy. Although his tragedy happened at the ripe age of thirty, he was so at peace with himself, it was almost as if he knew that day would be his last. I can't help but believe he was an angel walking among us, brought here to help others understand a greater way of life. It's been years since he left his mark on this wonderful world, yet his spirit continues to live in the hearts of others—and that my sea-loving friend, is how you become an unforgettable legend!

After receiving this infamous wake-up call, my entire outlook on life shifted. Through his death, I learned the impact you have on the people around you. I realized how everything could change in an instant, and I discovered what living to the fullest really boils down to. It's about taking chances, putting your passions to the test, turning every moment into a memory, having compassion for others, standing up for what you believe in and doing more of the stuff that makes you feel alive! I'm not here to tell you that life is short because I'm sure you know that by now. I'm here to help you make the most of your time and leave your mark of magic in this world so you too can continue to live on in the hearts of others, forever.

Create a Bucket List

If you are looking to fuel your life with purpose and fulfillment, I suggest you start making a bucket list STAT. With every adventure you cross off, comes a satisfying feeling of accomplishment. These once-in-a-lifetime experiences have the potential to nourish your spirit in ways unlike anything else. Having a bucket list gives you a crystal clear vision of the life you wish to lead by forcing you to sit down and really think about the milestones you dream of achieving. When you start thinking about what you really want to do, you can gain a new perspective on how you are currently spending your time versus how you *want* to spend your time. Some people want to travel the world solo, while others might choose to surround themselves with family. A bucket list doesn't have to consist of lavish and outlandish adventures, like jumping out of a plane, walking a red carpet, or swimming with dolphins in the wild. Your endeavors can be as simple as finishing a 1000-piece jigsaw puzzle, learning another language, or kissing someone in the rain.

When you sit down to write your list, recognize your values, remember your goals, and confront your fears. Let your fantasies run wild, and don't you dare hold back. Making a bucket list can help you tap into the imaginative side of you that dreams bigger, loves better, and doubts less. Then, once you've put the pen to paper and can recognize the experiences your heart hopes for, share these wishes with others or hang your list on the refrigerator with pride. That way, your everyday self can stay inspired to put those plans into action. You don't have to be at the tail end of your journey to start creating your bucket list either. In my opinion, the sooner you start taking note of your dream expeditions and encounters, the sooner you can start making the most of your life!

Respect Your Elders

One of my all time favorite books is the timeless classic *Tuesdays With Morrie* by Mitch Albom. It's a touching read about an old college professor and a curious student who meet every Tuesday for class. Spoiler Alert: Morrie is diagnosed with a terminal illness and continues to teach Albom every week from his deathbed. Except, instead of working together on a Masters thesis, Morrie lectures him about life's greatest lessons.

I know this sounds like a sappy fictional novel or potential Matthew McConaughey movie, but this sweet story unfolded in real life. Albom showed up every week, taking notes on what Morrie thought truly mattered when we reach "the end." He then turned it into a best-selling book that has changed millions of people's perspectives, mine included. Not only did this book help me become more comfortable with the idea of death, it also urged me to learn more from my elders. I know a lot of us struggle with having others tell us what we should and shouldn't do, but grandma always knows best, and so does the wise woman waiting at the bus stop. I mean, even the old geezer sipping on scotch at the bar has some life lessons to share.

Making an effort to be in the company of older generations will give you wisdom far beyond your years. People who have swum around the block a few times can provide guidance when you feel lost, and fill you with faith when all you feel is fear. Treat them with dignity and respect. Give up your seat, hold the door open for them, walk with them across the street, help load their groceries, ask them questions, and listen to their answers. Be kind and patient with every senior citizen because you'll eventually reach their age and walk in their shoes one day.

Growing old is a privilege and if you are lucky enough to experience your golden years, it is also your obligation to be a Morrie-type figure for the youth. Try your best to remember the lessons each life experience taught you, and share these transformational stories with the curious hearts willing to listen.

Embrace Your Age

Since we are on the topic of growing older, I have to ask, do you dig birthdays or despise them? It has become a societal norm for women to live in fear of aging. Some turn to plastic surgery procedures to preserve their youth, while others feel offended whenever they get asked, "How old are you?"

If you are doing everything in your power to hide laugh lines or find yourself hyperventilating whenever you spot a grey hair, it is time to stop with the Botox and embrace your silver fox. Maybe you have yet to find your first grey, but chances are you have experienced some anxiety at the thought of getting older.

I want you to know, there is no shame in your birthday game because how old you are does not define who you are. It is a number that represents how many years you have graced this earth with your presence. Do not let the wrinkles, hair loss, or under-eye circles make you feel bad about maturing. Life should be about the experiences, evolution, and improvement that all happen overtime.

Let's take a hot minute to think about who you were five years ago, shall we? Perhaps you were a broke student living off ramen noodles, dating total duds, and dancing on bar tops, crying for attention. Sure, your metabolism was way faster and hangovers were non-existent, but if you look beyond the physical traits and pay more attention to how your demeanor once was, you will see the young, naïve, and lost soul you really were. Although remaining forever young sounds ideal, when you think about it, it is way more of an ordeal. If you were to stay twenty-one until the end of time, then you would always be as reckless as you were at that age. Aging is not just about the physical breakdown; more importantly, it is about personal growth. Regardless of how old or young you may be now, it is necessary to welcome each year of life with open arms for the newfound knowledge and radical changes they bring.

It is also crucial that you do not use your age as a timeline for where you should be in your life. It is okay if you are in your late twenties and still in school; it is okay if you are in your thirties and still not married; it is even okay if you are forty-something, still living with mom and dad. We are all on our own agenda. Some of us are late bloomers while others of us are early developers. Trust that you will reach your monumental milestones when the timing is right, so stop worrying about what everyone else your age is doing and continue growing with grace.

Do What Makes You Feel Alive

There I was, paralyzed in savasana after what was, quite possibly, one of the most intense yoga classes I had ever taken. My heart was pounding out of my chest while my breath was roaring as loud as the ocean. I am not sure if it was the one hundred-degree heat making me delusional or if I somehow ignited that mind, body, spirit high yoga teachers are always preaching about. Either way, I have never felt more awakened than I did on the floor of that steamy yoga studio. In that very moment, I made a personal promise to do more of the stuff that makes me feel alive. Because let me tell you, that sensation was unlike any other. When was the last time you found yourself in a situation that made your stomach turn, heart race, or knees shake? I'm talking about an incident where you burst out into tears for no reason or laughed so hard that you peed your pants.

Although we have been trained by society to avoid such feelings, these are the kind of emotions that make us feel *alive*. It's healthy to get your adrenaline stirring while making the butterflies in your belly flutter because these natural reactions are the ultimate reminder you are living life to the fullest! Anytime you find yourself trembling with nerves or have chills shoot through your spine, lean into the discomfort. You were brought here to feel all the feels including fear, pain, and sadness. Without this emotional excitement, then what would be the point of existing?

Have Crystal Clear Values

Values play a major role in our behavior and serve as a reflection of what is important to us. When we have a deep understanding of the beliefs we keep close to our hearts, we are more inclined to make choices that align with these core values, leading us to experience life from a place of authenticity and integrity. But here is the catch—our family, friends, or even our community cannot determine these guiding principles. We must decide them. The influence of others can get us all caught up in what we think we should value rather than taking the time to figure out our own ways of thinking. Although it might seem like picking up on the values of our various social circles is unavoidable, it is our job to take a step back and judge these views for ourselves. We must make sure our internal code of conduct supports our true selves. So how does one become crystal clear on her personal values?

+ **Make a List**

   The first thing you are going to do is get in a quiet, secluded space and scribble out every value that speaks to your soul. Keep it short and sweet, limiting your list to ten, maybe fifteen, words max. That way, you are not overwhelmed trying to live up to every expectation and can connect with each idea.

+ **Define Their Meaning**

   After you shine light on what values matter most to you, take the time to understand why. What do these personal principles represent, and what are the reasons they hold significance for you? This tactic will bring more awareness to the values you have been taught by outside influences, compared to the values you have chosen for yourself.

+ **Prioritize Their Value**

Once you can comprehend the value behind your values, it is time to arrange them based on their significance. Prioritizing your principles ensures the beliefs you hold close to your heart never become compromised, allowing you to discover which ones are essential to your happiness, and which ones you can live without.

+ **Check-in with Yourself**

As you become crystal clear on your core values and realize why they are beneficial to you, be sure to keep your list close at hand. That way, you are constantly reminded to live in alignment with the core of your truth. Always check in with your choices and remember, as you continue to evolve, so will your values. Practice this method once a year to reevaluate your moral code and remain true to your internal ideals.

Make More Mistakes

Is it just me, or do mistakes have a way of haunting us? Sometimes, I suffer from symptoms of PTSD when I think about the moments I messed up. Like the time I tripped on stage at the Miss Hawaii U.S.A. pageant or when I drunk-dialed a babe from the gym, who just so happened to be a pitcher for the San Francisco Giants!

Whenever we step up to the plate with an opportunity and strike out swinging, we become consumed by feelings of shame, guilt, and embarrassment. These ego-crushing errors are why we prefer to play it safe in our comfort zones rather than take risks and potentially knock it out of the park. We pressure ourselves into perfectionism, which in the long run, only holds us back from moving forward. Let us not forget, we are trying to reach big league status here. If you are looking to go down like a legend then you have to be willing to make more mistakes, regardless of how agonizing the aftermath may be. Here is why your wrongdoings help you get closer to the hall of fame.

+ **Style of Learning**

    It may not be the traditional way to go about learning, but allowing more room for mistakes is an admirable way to learn. With some trial and error, you can understand what is, and what is not, working out anymore in your life. The consequences of our mistakes usually keep us from repeatedly making the same bad decisions.

+ **Healthy Way to Practice Self-Compassion**
It is incredibly easy to blame yourself every time things don't go as planned. Whenever you find your mind chiming in with negative chatter, it is urgent to take a time out and show yourself some compassion. Do not let your inner mean girl get the best of you. She is just a perfectionist trying to sabotage you. Mistakes are unavoidable, so you might as well permit yourself to mess up. Then, forgive your actions and move forward with more love in your heart than before.

+ **Build Resilience**
Making mistakes has a way of challenging you to bounce back after each setback. Do not throw yourself a pity party and play victim to the situation, but push yourself to be more determined than you were before. To persevere through those frustrating feelings of failure, you must own up to your errors and be proud of yourself for even trying. So the next time you find yourself falling flat on your face or ruining your shot with a professional baseball player, I want you to remember what the legendary

Babe Ruth once said, "Every strikeout brings me closer to my next home run."

Be a Wildcard

In the game of life, a wild card is someone who plays by her own rules. These individuals are confident characters that take risky chances, believing the odds are in their favor. They are unpredictable, untamed, and maybe even a little unsettled. But you know what? Who cares!

Wildcards do what they want when they want to do it. They are societal rebels with a "surprise!" mentality, showing up in the most unexpected of circumstances. They like to cause a little trouble, have a little fun, and don't care about consequences.

This mermaid is definitely a wildcard, but more importantly, you are, too. Together we form an unconventional tribe, redefining success by our values. We challenge the perspective of traditional thinking, and find fulfillment in paving the way for an unconventional future. So now that you know what a wildcard is, I want to touch base on the most important rule of this playful scheme: There are no rules! When it boils down to it, we all know this game of life will eventually come to an end. Why allow boring burdens to keep us from fully enjoying the experience? Stir up some trouble, make the somber smile, and play some epic jokes on your friends. Do what you want to do, whenever you want to do it.

Inspire, Don't Influence

Is it just me, or is everyone today on a mission to become a full-time influencer? I have to admit, I used to dream of getting paid to post something on social media . . . until I realized how meaningful it is to influence others. With this change of perception, I was able to recognize my ability to inspire people for the long-term, rather than persuade them into buying a detox tea for twenty percent off. Although, many might believe you need a couple hundred thousand followers to garner influence over others, it really boils down to the truth that the skill to inspire is within us all. You don't have to be a world-renowned motivational speaker or a verified content creator on Instagram to be considered an inspiration. All you need is to lead by example with a more thoughtful approach.

+ **Share Your Struggles**

   There is not a single person on earth who is not dealing with some kind of conflict. Opening up and sharing your struggles will make you real and relatable, allowing you to connect with others on a deeper level. Not only does it release some of the burdens you have been carrying around, it gives others comfort in knowing they are not alone. The only way to inspire friends, family, and strangers in such a courageous way is by breaking down your walls. To the outside eye, your life might seem ideal, but when you show others it is okay not to be okay, they become inspired by your ability to overcome difficult situations.

+ **Play by the Golden Rule**

The cool thing about treating everyone with kindness is the chain reaction it has over others. Doing one good deed for a friend will encourage them to return the favor with someone else because they were inspired by your small act of kindness. Always be on the lookout for moments to exchange a smile, hold the door open, or give a compliment. This kind of generosity is what lifts us up, motivates us, and pushes us to do more both for ourselves and for others.

+ **Maintain Integrity**

There is a big difference between doing versus spewing. Following through with what you say you are going to do is how you earn the respect and praise of your peers. When you keep the promises you make to others, as well as the promises you make to yourself, you are building a foundation of trust, authenticity, and reliability within all relationships. No one is inspired by the kind of people that sit on their butts and talk about their dreams; we are inspired by the kind of people who are out there chasing them down—the ones who make it happen, regardless of what is standing in their way. Integrity is the core value of every great leader, and leaders are chosen to guide, influence and instill inspiration in us all.

+ **Be of Service to Others**

The best way to inspire another individual is to give without any expectation of reciprocation. You have a unique skill to offer, whether it's a listening ear, your peaceful energy, sincere advice, or even the ability to make a mean margarita. Using your diverse talents to enhance the lives of others will result in a kind of connection that will leave them feeling seen, heard, understood, and appreciated. This style of heart-centered giving is love in its purest form, which in turn fills others with hope, comfort, and a deep desire to do the same.

+ **Remember Their Names**

There are a rare few who possess the remarkable talent to actually remember people's names after they introduce themselves. Unfortunately, I am not one of those people, but you know what? I am working on it, and you should, too! Having the savviness to remember a name makes others feel special. It shows them you are listening to what they say and genuinely care about who they are.

+ **Do You Boo**

   Being an inspiration to others has a way of fulfilling us, but the only person you should be worried about inspiring is yourself. When you have a genuine enthusiasm for the life you live, people are drawn to you. They appreciate your energy, they admire your independence, and they ask for your advice. Ironically, inspirational leaders do not tell people what they should do; they show them. Focus on being the best you that you can be, and watch as others feel influenced to follow your lead rather than your Instagram account.

Turn Moments into Memories

They say when staring at the face of death, life flashes before your eyes. Now, I am not sure if that is entirely true, but I do know that your life is made up of a series of memories. As a matter of fact, your conscious recollections have helped shape you into the mermaid you are today. Your worldview, values, and opinions are all based on experiences you have encountered at some point in your life. Some have the power to pull at your heartstrings and leave you feeling all kinds of nostalgic, while others are a bit more complicated—helping you learn, grow, and even change the entire direction of your life.

When you think about it, our memories are fascinating because they require a different kind of brainpower than what it takes to memorize a script or remember what you had for lunch the other day. The forever kind of memories are connected to our emotions and have the power to take us back to a place and time, as if it was yesterday. Whether you sort through your shoebox of old photos, read your collection of journals, or utilize your Facebook timeline, everyone looks back in her own way. But let's say you are one of the many individuals who prefer not to dwell in the past. Maybe you do not see the point in reminiscing on "the good 'ole days." That is okay—to each her own. Just do not come crying to me when the time comes to share your most treasured moments with the people closest to you and struggle to get sentimental. Our memories not only fill our life with meaning, they also keep us alive in the hearts of others long after we leave this mortal realm.

Even though my grandpa passed before I was born, I still feel a strong connection to the man every time I hear stories about his circus days. That's right—I am a direct descendant of a circus freak. Actually, he was more of a circus stud since his infamous act involved riding around in the cage of death alongside seven other motorcycles. I think it is safe to say his enthusiasm for entertainment lives within me, but I would have never known this fun fact if Grandpa Shorty didn't live life in such a legendary way!

Despite my grandfather's daredevil demeanor, you do not need to run away and join the circus with the hopes of making memories that will last a lifetime. You just have to take some chances, explore different passions, surround yourself with the people you love, and take note of the special moments that make your heart sing.

Spread Your Light

As I write this book, the current situation of our world is in distress. With global pandemics, sexual discrimination, tragic shootings, and endless political protests, we have been facing some tough times. Granted, as you read this, present-day conditions may be a bit better, but history always has a way of repeating itself.

As devastating as these catastrophes have been, I believe it is our purpose as spiritual beings to be a ray of light amidst the darkest of times. Deep within you is a radiant glow that has the power to bring warmth, comfort, and hope to the world around you. It is similar to lighting the candles on a birthday cake. With a single flame, you can light up as many candles as you need without ever diminishing the original flame. I want you to consider yourself an OG candle and imagine sparking others with your kindness, compassion, trust, and sympathy. These are the qualities that make up your internal glow, and you have to let them shine! Do not get swallowed up in the shadows, but rather, step into your full potential and start to share your light with the people that need it most.

LIVE.

I can't help but feel as if my life began, the moment Sean's life ended. Through his passing I was able to see how it can all be over in the blink of an eye and I became inspired to live in a way that would make him proud. If you already know that tomorrow is never promised, then why shouldn't you go out there and seize the day? We are only here on this planet for a minuscule amount of time, and to be honest, it is kind of amazing that we are even here today. Stop trying to avoid the truth and age with grace. Stop spending money on material goods and start spending time making memories. Stop avoiding the pain and start learning from mistakes. Stop pleasing societal standards and start playing by your own rules. Stop worrying about what comes after death, and start doing what you can to make the most of this one life!

In the wise words of Mr. Moses, "This is your time, LIVE."

Chapter 8

Never Grow Up, Never Give Up

*B*etween the endless tears and hand-me-down clothes, you can imagine how being raised with three tormenting brothers was a constant struggle in my mermaid youth. I will never forget the day my parents rounded up the troops for a delightful dip in the pool. Similar to every other tiny tot born during *The Little Mermaid* era, I used to mimic the Disney idol of our generation. I loved to play pretend by flipping my fins around and holding my breath for as long as my little lungs would allow.

During that unforgettable day of family play, I was attempting to recreate that legendary wave-crashing scene from the movie. You know . . . the one where Ariel is sitting on a rock, daydreaming about Prince Eric during the "Part of Your World" grand finale. On my attempt to surface back to land, I pushed up against the edge of the pool, fantasizing about my prince charming while a roaring, rogue wave crashed behind me. Struggling to flip my fins in the chlorinated water as the top half of my body breached on the concrete, I eagerly asked my brothers, "Do I look like a mermaid?"

With no hesitation those quick-witted jerks responded, "More like Shamu."

As insulting as it was being compared to a 6,000-pound whale, I didn't let their perfect punch line get to me. These guys were constantly challenging me with their loving words of discouragement. Still to this day, they manage to harass me with their sarcasm. And still to this day, I don't let it phase me. I appreciate it because their brotherly love is the reason for my resilience. Now that I have transitioned into my "grown up" years, it is sort of surreal how I never gave up on my dream of becoming a mermaid. Regardless of the people who joked, teased, and doubted, I did it. Despite how crazy it sounded or unstable the path would be, I did it. Looking back at the time between, I can see how the journey shaped me into the glowing spirit I am today, and how The Universe conspired to turn this frivolous five-year-old dream into a full-blown reality.

There is something special about that innocence to dream without a doubt in the world. Yet, somewhere along the lines of childhood and #adulting, we are told to grow up and forced to give up our whimsical wishes. Not because we need to, but because we start living to please everyone else's expectations. We go to college to make our parents happy, we stay at our torturous job because it makes us seem successful, and we feel obligated to start a family because it is what everyone else is doing.

For some strange reason, it is almost as if the older we get the more we lose touch with our genuine selves. We put on a show to look prim and proper, yet deep down, our souls crave to be wild and free. Our ideas and imagination often seem silly to mature minds, so in hopes of fitting in, we keep our desires quiet. Playtime takes a backseat to errands and everyday stresses keep us from enjoying the simple pleasure of an ice cream cone. Our ability to create drawings and poems somehow disappear as we become consumed by the pressure of perfection. We avoid asking questions and seeking new knowledge since as adults, we are expected to have it all figured out. And we believe it is too late in life to go out there and become the person we have always dreamed of being. It is almost as if the farther away we wander from that sense of childlike wonder, the farther away we remain from having a joyous and magical life.

With that being said, I am dying to know, would your five-year-old self be happy with the way you are currently living? Are you doing your best to make that mini-mermaid proud, or do you not really remember much of her? It is okay if you lost yourself along the way from then to now. Prioritizing responsibility is a part of getting older, but staying connected to your inner-child is how to prevent yourself from growing up.

There is no doubt in my mind that if I went back in time to chat with a mini version of me, that curly haired cutie would be in complete awe of the mermaid I am today. The reason I can say that with such certainty is because at this point in my life, I can see a look of admiration in the eyes of my brothers. These boys have witnessed my mermaid transformation first-hand. Watching me grow from dreamer to believer, staying true to my vision without any intention to throw in the towel. Although as kids, they were always teasing and taunting, I am the one who gets the last laugh because as adults, they have become my biggest supporters. Thanks to my relentless determination, my enthusiastic spirit, and my everlasting connection to this impractical dream, they can recognize me for the mermaid I am today. When you reach the age where phrases like, "Welcome to the real world" and "It's time to grow up" lead you toward the dullness of #adulting, I have learned it's crucial to color your life outside of the lines if you ever want to find your happily ever after. Here is how to avoid growing up and giving up on the mini-mermaid within.

Remember Your Roots

Can you recall some of your best days as a child? Do you remember your favorite Saturday morning cartoons, playing tag at recess, or chasing down the ice cream truck for an afternoon snack? Did you try out for any sports? Who were your friends, and what did you do for fun? It is time to take a time out and reflect on where you came from.

Lucky for me, my pops was obsessed with his video camera and pretty much recorded my entire childhood. Whenever it is time to gather around with the family and watch those classic home videos, I can recognize the parts of myself that make me who I am today. I notice how I have always been a fan of the spotlight, I can see my grit comes from that brotherly "love," and it's reassuring to recognize I have always had quite the imagination.

Flipping through your photo books, looking at past school projects, visiting the home where you grew up, or re-reading old journals are rad ways to reminisce on your childhood. Try sitting down with your parents and asking them to tell you tales of a point in time you were too young to remember. Taking a walk down memory lane is like retracing your steps on this journey and reconnecting with the core of who you were before outside influences and internal doubt told you who to be. When you look back, you will notice different clues to where your true passions lay and gain new insight on quirky qualities that have always been a part of you! Make an effort to reconnect with those sentimental memories more frequently by remembering your roots and recognizing how much you have grown through the years.

Pencil in Play Dates

Spending time with kids is definitely worth your while. They are not just good at saying the darnedest things; they also have a way of challenging your imagination and keeping your perspective fresh. One of my best friends is a six-year-old named Madilynn. This little lady means the world to me, partly because she thinks I am a teenager (bless her heart), but mainly because she helps keep my imagination sharp. She is not afraid to give me her honest answer or tell me what is really on her mind. She finds joy in little things, such as the farting noise out of a whoopee cushion. She also has a way of reminding me that sugar rushes are a real thing.

With their pure hearts and playful energy, kids are a refreshing break from reality. They give us a chance to take a step back and reconnect with the mischievous, creative, cheerful side within us. They help us see the world from a fresh perspective every time they spot something for the first time. Have you ever seen a kid get excited over a blimp or a butterfly? How can you not smile at that kind of enthusiasm?

If you have a tiny tot in your life, keep them close. Make more of an effort to spend quality time with them. Schedule in play dates, surprise them with ice cream, or take them to an amusement park. I can guarantee this relationship will be one of the most rewarding ones you will ever have, and you might be surprised to see how much you can learn from each other.

Cultivate Curiosity

Philosophical smarty-pants people, including Alan Watts, Eleanor Roosevelt, and Mr. Walt Disney himself have all preached the importance of questions. Curiosity is not only a key characteristic of children; it is also a fundamental trait of mermaids. Children wander through their youth constantly experiencing a natural state of questioning. Although the constant cry of "Why? Why? Why?" can test your patience as an adult, you gotta love it because these munchkins genuinely want to know why the sky is blue, why we have belly buttons, and *why* they can't eat the play-dough!

Keeping the brain stimulated is a lifelong task that often gets pushed aside the older we get. As we age, it is common to lose our sense of speculation due to our insecurities of looking foolish. Somehow, we have it ingrained in our brains that as adults, we are supposed to have it all figured out. But I've got news for you sea sister! No one has it figured out, not even those infamous intellects. Which is probably why they had a hunger for learning and spent their precious time preaching the importance of questions!

Strengthening your sense of curiosity can lead to some serious personal development, as well as help you reach new levels within your career. However, nurturing your appetite for answers requires more than merely asking questions; it is also about overcoming the worry of appearing ignorant to others. With all the wisdom we can hold in the palms of our hands (hello Google), there is no reason why we should not be doing the research and finding the answers to our questions. Bonus points for embracing the vulnerability by asking someone for the answer, and double bonus points if you take your vulnerability to the next level and ask questions to learn about your fellow mer-people.

Cultivating a spirit of curiosity does more than make you smarter, it also has the power to bring you closer to other individuals. Together you can learn, grow, and always wonder, "Why?"

Face Your Fears

Some of us are scared of heights; some of us are scared of spiders; some of us are even scared of dating (or maybe that's just me). Either way, what I'm trying to say is—*we all have our fears*. We've experienced eerie encounters that make our hearts race, stomachs turn, and breaths grow shallow. But rather than embrace these feelings, we flee from them with the intention to protect ourselves. We avoid climbing mountains, scream for help when we see a spider, and ghost a guy to steer clear of vulnerability. Then as a result, we stay in our cushy, comfort zones, never allowing ourselves to overcome the freight.

Fear is a weird emotion because sometimes, it protects us from danger, and other times, it helps us experience courage. You can't be brave if you don't push through the fear that you are feeling. On the other side of your fear is where you build strength, tenacity, and spunk.

The adult in me almost forgot how fearless kids really are until one of my many days spent people watching on the beach. As I sat there observing my surroundings, a fearless little dude caught my eye as he heroically climbed the ledge of a five-foot wall. In my paranoid mind, I was already imagining all the incidences that could have gone wrong in that moment. Is he going to fall? Will there be blood? Where are his parents? Yet, this brave kid was not scared one bit. He scaled that ledge of that wall with confidence, each step taking him higher and higher away from the ground. Then, with little hesitation he jumped off the ledge crashing face first into the sand. Once his D.I.L.F. of a dad came to the rescue, he shook off the sand and climbed right back up, scaling the wall all over again with even more pep in his step. The continuous action of climbing and falling went on for several attempts, until another baby BASE jumper watched in awe. Eventually, the other one worked up enough courage to join in on the fearless fun, and together they jumped off the ledge with audacity.

Kids are intuitive beings. They can exist without worry because A) Their parents can pick them up when they fall, and B) They live strictly in the moment. As we transition into adulthood, fear is often triggered by imagining all the potential *should* have, *would* have, *could* have moments. Sitting there on the beach and watching those kids faceplate into the sand frightened my mind with the possibility of what could go wrong. But fear plays off the future, and the last thing kids worry about is what will happen next.

Now I want you to take a second and think about something you have always wanted to do. Whether it's traveling the world with nothing but the comfort of a backpack, quitting your steady job to take a chance on your own successful business, or maybe even signing the lease to your very own (and very expensive) apartment. Next, rather than surrendering to the fears of all the potential ways your dream could go wrong, flip the switch, and begin to manifest the doors of possibilities that could potentially open. This tactic will help you respond with confidence to the naysayers.

Our dreams often remain dreams because when we choose to share them with our closest friends and family, in hopes of acquiring support, their initial reaction is not ideal. But remember, they, too, may be simply ignoring their childlike curiosity and trying to make sense of someone who is confident enough to take an intimidating chance on the unknown. Then, as they watch you begin to fearlessly scale across the wall toward your dream, they will look at you in awe and eventually work up the courage to join in on all the fearless fun!

Sharing is Caring

In our younger years, we are rewarded for sharing our toys, appreciated for sharing our food, and sometimes forced to share our rooms. We were taught that sharing is caring . . . until the day came when we had to cook our own meals, move out into our own houses, and start to buy our own toys. As if sharing wasn't already hard enough, when we transition into adulthood, it becomes even more of a challenge. Instead of sharing clothes with our sister or sharing a car with our little brother, we are asked to share our money, expected to share our time, and obligated to share our energy.

This mature march toward big-time sharing is more about giving ourselves rather than giving our things.

When we stop to think about it, we are all in this together. Sharing as an adult connects us to a community, teaches us how to trust, and helps us be more cooperative since it is a two-way street. Meaning, it is pretty much impossible to share without another person receiving on the other end. Regardless of how old we are, we don't ever grow out of sharing with others. Let's always show them how much we care about their needs by giving them a little bit of ourselves!

Celebrate the Little Things

What I would give to do Kindergarten all over again. From what I recall, most of that class time was spent learning the ABCs, running relay races at recess, and painting masterpieces using only my fingers. And those were not even close to being the best parts about Kinder class.

What I cherished most about this monumental grade was that I was still given a gold star, even though my letters were written backwards. I still managed to earn a participation medal, even if I was the slowest runner in school. And my artwork was still displayed on the fridge, despite how hard it was to look at.

As kids, it didn't matter how good you were at something, your efforts were always rewarded, honored, and celebrated. Yet, for some strange reason, it's more of a struggle to have the same kind of pride for accomplishments as an adult. We let the stress of perfection and fear of judgment keep us from creating freely. Regardless of how hard you try, it can feel like your work isn't valuable enough to hang on the fridge or brag about at show and tell. The amount of pressure we put on ourselves as we age is pretty insane. It's time to give yourself a gold star for simply showing up and doing the work. Your efforts deserve to be praised, regardless of the outcome. Be proud of yourself for all that you try, all that you do, and all that you are.

Growth is Everlasting

Newborn babies are beautiful in their own way. By beautiful, I mean kind of creepy. (There, I said it.) Although this truth might come off as harsh, you have to admit, newborns look eerily similar to baby aliens until the growth process starts to kick in. Inch by inch these little babes start to get taller, sprout silky strands of hair, and grow a precious set of teeth the size of Tic Tacs.

Then, in the blink of an eye, they turn into teenagers and get all kinds of awkward. Not just from the braces and acne, but also from the new parts of their bodies that are starting to blossom. Eventually, after years go by, what used to look like a shriveled, fuzzy caterpillar has transformed into a butterfly, ready to share its beauty with the world. Hopefully by this point in life, you have lost all your baby teeth, become tall enough to ride your favorite roller coaster, and survived puberty.

However, just because your body is now fully developed, doesn't mean you are done growing. Your soul is always seeking to evolve. And just like the achy bones that come with any growth spurt, personal progress can be just as agonizing. To experience growth as an adult, you have to be willing to step out of your comfort zone by letting go of your old ways. You must seek out constructive criticism to recognize where there is room for improvement, and you need to practice patience with the process. You didn't become the gorgeous being you are today overnight. You had to go through your awkward alien phase first. Growth takes time, courage, and a never-ending commitment to yourself. Continue trusting the transformation, because regardless of how old you become, your soul is constantly growing.

Heal Your Heart

As you can tell by my mortifying Shamu story, I dealt with a lot of emotional abuse as a child. I was constantly teased about my weight as a kid, and it triggered my binging habit as an adult. Growing up with a lack of affection in my family has made it tougher to for me to show love. Sorry to be airing out my dirty laundry, but I am just trying to be real over here.

Whether you realize it or not, there are past traumas and tribulations from your childhood that you are still hanging on to after all these years. Emotional wounds from our youth have been buried deep in our bones, and as children we were unaware of how to deal with them. These past traumas look different to everyone, ranging from physical abuse and emotional neglect to losing someone special or surviving a natural disaster. When our hearts are damaged during developmental stages, it makes it easy to put up walls and harder to find the healing that we need to feel whole again. The impact these life-altering situations have can lead to negative effects on our emotional, psychological, and physiological wellbeing. Healing these invisible wounds can be heavy on the heart, but the best way to get over the past is to start by facing it one step at a time.

+ **Get Honest**

   Admitting to yourself that you are not okay is the first step in healing your heart. It can be terrifying AF to face the parts of yourself that you struggle with, but you have to get honest with where your issues lie if you ever want to move past the trauma. Ask yourself the tough questions, listen to what your emotions are telling you, and try to remember moments when those same feelings were triggered.

+ **Let Your Walls Down**

   Every time you encounter something traumatic, more bricks are placed on your metaphorical wall. Pain is caused, trust is lost, and barriers are built to prevent the situation from happening again. I know this kind of survival mode might sound like a good idea, but pushing people away is not the answer. I encourage you to let your guard down and share stories with people about what you went through. Getting it off your chest will cause your heart to feel lighter, and you just might be able to save someone struggling with a similar situation.

+ **Release Resistance**

These past wounds have a way of living in our bodies. Since we did not understand how to process the emotions as a child, we tend to bury the feelings deep in our bones. Pay attention to where you feel resistance in the body, and then breathe into those areas, and imagine yourself letting go of the tension you have been hanging on to all these years. Stretch it out, open it up, and heal from the trauma by creating space for new energy to enter the body.

+ **Move Forward**

The final step toward your healing process is moving forward. You have to understand that the pain you are feeling is from something that happened in the past. You cannot change it, you had no control over it, and you should not torture yourself because of it. When you can comprehend what happened from a mature mindset, you will have new insight and awareness as to what happened and why. Healing takes time so be patient with yourself as you continue on from a place of love and light.

Always Believe in Magic

I believed in Santa and the Tooth Fairy longer then I am proud to admit. Like most youngsters, I would stay up into the wee hours of the evening, hoping to catch a glimpse of these make-believe characters. Until my brothers, yet again, burst my bubble by giving me a sneak peek of our Christmas presents hiding in the closet. Although I felt a slight betrayal from my parents, who lied to me for all those years, as an adult, I can understand they were just trying to protect my childhood innocence for as long as possible. When we figure out that jolly St. Nick is, in fact, a ho-ho-ho hoax, life begins to lose its wonder.

For some of us, this revelation drives us to become skeptical toward the outside world and jaded when it comes to believing in the magic of possibility. I might have thought Santa was real well into my double digits, but it beats being the kid that spoils it for everyone. Every time I entertain at a birthday party, there is always a non-believer that calls me out for being a fraud. They don't just poke fun at my every move, they also say, "You aren't real." Flat out, just like that (and I thought my brothers were bad).

Around the time kids grow out of their fascination with fantasy, is also around the time they stop dreaming and start doubting. Their imagination grows dull as they find joy in ruining the fun for everyone else! Fortunately, believing in Santa for so long taught me to never break character. I feel like it's my duty, every time I take the stage as a mermaid, to keep the magic alive for the little ones who do believe.

It is crucial to protect your childhood wonder for as long as possible to keep your perspective fresh and spirit free. You do not have to convince yourself that unicorns, leprechauns, and the Easter Bunny are real. You just have to reconnect with the part of yourself that is able to dream, imagine, and believe that anything is possible!

The Best is Yet To Come

Even though it might feel like your best years are behind you, the way I see it, you are just getting started sea sister! How exciting is it to know that some of life's greatest moments have yet to happen? Don't get too set in your ways or start to think your prime time is long gone because the truth is, you still have so much more to experience.

Life is an endless creation of who you are and who you wish to become.

In your hands lie all the tricks of the mermaid trade. You now know what you need to do to care for your mind, body, and spirit. You have learned how to make play a priority, bounce back after defeat, and dream like you are five years old all over again. You have developed a stronger connection to The Universe, changed your perspective on death, and understand what it takes to make every day fabulous! Now, it is up to you to believe with all your heart that you are worthy, deserving, and able to transform into the best version of you. Put these practices to good use, and allow yourself to radiate like the blissful being you were born to be! With the newfound insight, guidance, and motivation this book has provided, it is time for you to go out there and start living the life you have always dreamed of! Sure, there will be moments when you find yourself drowning in the stresses of responsibility, intimidated by cold, dark uncertain waters, or feel lost out at sea. But I promise, if you do your best to stick with this magical method and live each day to your fullest potential, life will become better than you could ever imagine!

Trust me, I'm a mermaid.

And now you are, too.

About the Author

Gennah Nicole is a Certified Wellness Coach and Professional Mermaid on a mission to help women of all ages unleash the glowing spirit within. Her motivational writing has been featured on *FabFitFun*, *Thought Catalog*, and *DISfunkshion* magazine.

When she isn't busy writing books and entertaining as a mermaid, you can find her running marathons, making margaritas, collecting seashells, or catching the sunset.

For more guidance, visit themermaidmethod.com or follow her on social media @gennahnicole.

CPSIA information can be obtained
at www.ICGtesting.com
Printed in the USA
JSHW021507150521
14795JS00001B/17

9 781631 953156